REKINDLING WONDER

TOUCHING HEAVEN IN A SCREEN SATURATED WORLD

Fr. Christopher J. Seith

En Route Books and Media, LLC
St. Louis, MO

⊕ ENROUTE
Make the time

En Route Books and Media, LLC
5705 Rhodes Avenue
St. Louis, MO 63109

Cover credit: Joni J. Seith,
from Raphael's *Transfiguration* (1520)

ISBN-13: 978-1-956715-84-2
Library of Congress Control Number: 2022946573

Copyright © 2022 Fr. Christopher J. Seith
All rights reserved.

No part of this booklet may be reproduced, stored in a retrieval system, or transmitted in any form, or by any means, electronic, mechanical, photocopying, or otherwise, without the prior written permission of the author.

Dedication

Because our Lady never tires of hearing of the love her priests have for her, I join my own poor voice to the voices of all those who have dedicated their work to her, without whom the world would never have seen the Radiant Beauty of the Incarnate God.

Acknowledgments

This book has been the fruit of many years' work and was only made possible by the prayers and support of many people.

I have to begin with an impossible task, that of expressing my gratitude to my family. Without the love of my saintly mother and father, my sister and her family, and my brothers, I would not have known Christ's power to manifest the fullness of Life in the midst of very real suffering. From you I learned, by experience, the truth of John Paul II's words: "Prayer joined to sacrifice constitutes the most powerful force in human history." Without you, this book would have been nothing but abstract ideas rather than a reflection of lived experience.

I must also thank the priests of the Archdiocese of Washington and the seminarians of John Paul II Seminary, who had to endure random outbursts of excitement or heartbreak during my time of writing this book. Your reciprocal excitement and heartbreak on the topic confirmed my hope that what I was writing would benefit others. In particular, I have to thank Bishop William Byrne, Fr. Carter Griffin, Fr. Kevin Regan, Fr. Mark Ivany, Fr. Conrad

Murphy, Fr. Martino Choi, Fr. Pat Lewis, Fr. Jamie Morrison, and Fr. Brendan Glasgow. Along with them are all of those who serve at the Institute for Priestly Formation. Thank you for the gift of your friendship and inspiring priestly witness.

I would be remiss if I did not single out the many consecrated religious sisters who helped inspire this book. In you is the image of the Bride of Christ, the radiance of a life wholly given to God. Your consecration stands in direct contrast to a profaned world and reminds us of our heavenly vocation. I cannot thank you enough for your witness. This book would not have been possible without you. In particular, I want to thank the Religious Sisters of Mercy of Alma, Michigan, the Sister Servants of the Lord, and the cloistered Dominican Sisters in Linden, VA.

Finally, there are so many people who helped in the editing of this book. First, I have to thank everyone at En Route Books & Media who took the risk of publishing a first-time author. Thank you to Fr. John Horn, SJ, for putting me in touch with Dr. Sebastian Mahfood, OP, and to Sebastian for your patience and care in working with me. I am so grateful to Dr. John Grabowski for directing my dissertation, which was basically a much more boring and tedious version of this book! Thank you also to Ben and Mary Szoch for reading early drafts of the book, and to Annie McHugh for reading the entire thing with a fine tooth comb! And again, thank you to my family for having read so many drafts that you could have written the book!

TABLE OF CONTENTS

Introduction 1

Chapter 1: Naming the Darkness 9

Chapter 2: Digital Seduction 37

Chapter 3: Light in a Land of Shadows 81

Chapter 4: Divine Conquest 111

Conclusion 139

Introduction

Years after writing *The Screwtape Letters*, C.S. Lewis imagined the famed demonic Tempter, Screwtape, offering a toast to a group of demons at the annual dinner of the "Tempters' Training College for young Devils."[1] In his toast, Screwtape laments the quality of their food. Naturally, they had been feasting on the souls of the damned. But Screwtape remarks that there was hardly any flavor in any of these souls. When Hell had feasted on the likes of a Hitler, the flavor of sin was overwhelming. But these souls? The poor wretches feeding the demons of Hell these days, according to Screwtape, are downright bland.

It is challenging to tell the story of contemporary man because, frankly, it is a boring story. A Hitler provides a fascinating (and horrifying!) story because his was the soul of a humanity egregiously destroyed.

---

[1] Cf. C.S. Lewis, "Screwtape Proposes a Toast" in *The Screwtape Letters with Screwtape Proposes a Toast* (New York: Harper One, 2015), 187-209.

He directed all the powers of his soul to the pursuit of evil. He gives the storyteller something remarkable with which to work. As for contemporary man, his is not the soul of a disfigured humanity but of a castrated humanity. The powers of his soul are not directed energetically toward evil because they are not directed at all. Who wants to hear the story of a man who passively moves from one task to the next until he finds himself on his deathbed surrounded by distractions? But so it is. This is more and more the story of the men and women of our age; incapable of providing the demons of Hell with culinary delight because they are equally incapable of delighting the eyes of Heaven. Our humanity has not been destroyed but numbed.

Of course, the demons have only themselves to blame for their bland fare. It is one of their own who brought about this sad state of affairs. In ancient Christianity, the desert fathers named the demon that made all things boring "the noonday devil."[2]

---

[2] Cf. Dom Jean-Charles Nault, O.S.B., *The Noonday Devil: Acedia, the Unnamed Evil of our Times*, trans.

This devil afflicted the soul with sadness for being made in the image and likeness of God. The soul so afflicted wishes he were less than human so as to avoid the challenging adventure inherent in his humanity - to radiate the self-giving love of God revealed in Jesus Christ. Thus saddened by what he is, man's life becomes, quite simply, boring.

In the following pages, I will argue that the noonday devil, also known as *acedia*, is not only the underlying spirit of our age, but that it also has a new and effective weapon: digital devices.[3] Admittedly, the use of these devices has not been without benefits. The capacity to stay connected with distant loved ones, the ease of looking up information of various kinds, and even the simple pleasure of watching an entertaining video are all beneficial activities.

But these devices have not been designed merely to be used but rather to be woven into the very fabric

---

Michael J. Miller (San Francisco: Ignatius Press, 2015), 21-105.

[3] I use the term "digital devices" with a certain intentional ambiguity to include the various distracting gadgets and screens with which we surround ourselves.

of our lives. Because of our screens' ubiquitous presence in the world, we have conformed our lives to these digital devices. It is not enough to have access to the Internet. We must be constantly connected - at work, at the dinner table, on the toilet. We must no longer think of ourselves as a being distinct from our digital devices. Transhumanists envision a world in which human brains are merged with computers. Whether or not that happens, it is already how we think of ourselves. *Using* the Internet? No, these devices do not ask us to use them; they demand that we conform our lives to them.

None of this would be particularly disturbing if it were not for the fact that by conforming ourselves to digital devices, we lose the capacity to find joy in reality. We think of the world as something that should adapt itself to us for our convenience. We should not need to *wait* for the next episode of a series to come out. We should not need to leave the house to pick up groceries. We should not need to wear pants during a work meeting. We should not even need to win the trust of the other to expect her to reveal herself in all her vulnerability. More and more, we think of reality as something available at our convenience. We become incapable of perceiving anything as having a life that is not under our control. Slowly but surely, conforming ourselves to these devices, we begin to scorn anything that might require relinquishing control in order for us to be in relationship with it.

And so it is that this most elusive of demons traps souls in its snare. Man's life, which finds its fulfillment in an act of self-forgetting love, becomes a source of sadness. We wish we were other than we are. We wish we could be the center of our lives and find fulfillment in ourselves rather than in another. Unbeknownst to us, we find that we have purchased the conveniences offered by our digital devices at the price of our soul. In the various forms that our devices take, *acedia* has found its most effective weapon to date.

There is something refreshing about becoming aware of one's own misery. Someone in chronic pain finds immense relief when he learns that his pain is real and has a cause. The same is true for spiritual misery. How relieving it is to name the despairing indifference that hovers like a fog over modern man. Psychological diagnoses, helpful and necessary as they are, cannot plumb the depths of modernity's ennui. Only the One who "knows what is in man" can reveal the sickness so crippling him: the sickness of having rejected the fullness of life in Christ.

When Jesus began his public ministry in Nazareth, he used the words of Isaiah to articulate his mission. "The Spirit of the Lord is upon me, because he has anointed me to preach good news to the poor. He has sent me to proclaim release to captives and recovery of sight to the blind, to set at liberty those who are oppressed, to proclaim the acceptable year of the Lord."[4] Jesus continues his mission in our day. He looks upon us and sees the oppression we experience because of our devices. And He has come to set captives free from the reign of the noonday devil. Christ invites us to live a new life, a life of festive joy celebrating what God has done in creating and redeeming the world. By looking to Jesus Christ and renouncing the allure of the world, we are set free from a life of boredom. No longer will our souls make demons gag. Rather, ours will be souls which fill them with hatred and fear, while shining like stars in the

---

[4] Luke 4:18-19. All Scripture references, unless otherwise noted, will be from the RSV translation.

sky in the midst of a darkened world. My hope is that this book will expose *acedia*'s lurking presence behind the screen and present the freedom that Christ offers us here and now. Christ's victory over Satan was not a one-time event that occurred 2,000 years ago. He continues to triumph over the various instantiations of Satan's tyranny which he now imposes through the use of our screens.

In his letter to the Romans, St. Paul prayed: "Do not be conformed to this world, but be transformed by the renewal of your minds, so that you may know what is God's will, what is good and pleasing and perfect."[5] This book was written with the same prayer in mind, that Jesus Christ may give us a new way of seeing reality and reveal to us the wondrous hope of life with Him. In this hope, we find the true antidote to our digital despair.

---

[5] Romans 12:1-2.

Chapter 1

Naming the Darkness

In J.R.R. Tolkien's *Lord of the Rings*, the author tells of an adventure in which a fellowship of nine companions is sent by an elven lord, Elrond, to destroy a ring. This ring, in the hands of the Enemy, has the power to cover all the world in darkness and despair by enslaving others' minds within the Enemy's mind. And indeed, even in the hands of the virtuous, the ring has the power to corrupt its bearers. As the fellowship makes its quest, they enjoy a period of respite in a peaceful land that is under the protection of an elven queen, Galadriel. One of the characters, Gimli, upon seeing the beauty of Galadriel, is absolutely smitten by her. She welcomes him so graciously that he is completely taken aback. When the time comes for the fellowship to depart from that land, he laments to his friend:

Tell me... why did I come on this Quest? Little did I know where the chief peril lay! Truly

> Elrond spoke, saying we could not foresee what we might meet upon our road. Torment in the dark was the danger that I feared, and it did not hold me back. But I would not have come, had I known the dangers of light and joy. Now I have taken my worst wound at this parting, even if I were to go this night straight to the Dark Lord.[6]

After having encountered the beauty of Galadriel, facing a world without her appears more painful than any tortures he could have imagined.

Gimli's experience is not foreign to us. We know it all too well. We fall in love and encounter someone whose beauty is overpowering. Even more, that beauty does not merely stand there to be admired, but reaches out and welcomes us into her presence. For a moment, we have the feeling that our life is about more than the drudgery of the workaday world, that our true home is the place where that beauty exists. But then the moment passes. Like

---

[6] J.R.R. Tolkien, *The Lord of the Rings: The Fellowship of the Ring* (New York: Ballantine Books, 1982), 446.

Chapter 1: Naming the Darkness

waking up from a dream, we return to the task at hand. Except now, the world without that beauty is even more difficult to face. We realize that we are exiles, doomed to live in a world separated from the beauty that makes us fully alive. As long as the memory of our encounter with beauty exists, our lives are consumed by longing. This is the danger, as Gimli puts it, "of light and joy."

This must have been the experience of those who encountered Jesus of Nazareth. When they saw Him, not only did they behold the beauty of God in the flesh, but *He* saw *them* and delighted in them. They beheld the very God who looked upon what He had created and cried out, "it is very good!" And that same God was now turning His approving gaze upon them, looking for them to simply receive His affirmation of their true dignity and have life because of it. No wonder the sick were healed simply at the touch of Jesus' hand. Does not even human love give us an increase of life and wholeness? How much more the love of Jesus? No wonder sinners so readily abandoned their former way of life. Seeing His gaze, those who met Jesus lived differently. They lived from that encounter and in longing for that encounter.

This "living differently," however, can take different forms. Having been wounded by longing for the gaze of Christ, we are now faced with two options. Either we live in joyful hope, confident that there are no vain desires, that the wound in our hearts will be healed; or we live in despairing sadness, wishing that we had never encountered such beauty. Those who choose the first option find themselves living, while still on earth, in the Kingdom of Heaven. They experience hardships and difficulties, pains and sorrows, yet always with the confidence that such afflictions are preparing for them an "eternal weight of glory beyond all comparison."[7] By contrast, those who choose the second option find themselves imprisoned in a different sort of kingdom. They, too, experience all the challenges of life in exile but they do so with a spirit of sadness. They refuse to live with the pain of longing and prefer, instead, to live with the pain of despair. Life for them becomes a foretaste of Hell.

---

[7] 2 Cor 4:17.

Chapter 1: Naming the Darkness

This "hell" is not some external punishment but is rather experienced interiorly as a diminishment of being. Those who refuse to long for heaven wish they were less than human so that they could be satisfied more easily. They grieve that they can only find fulfillment in love because such a destiny demands that they wait, in hope, for the beloved's gift of self. They cannot force it. And rather than living in hope of fulfillment, these sorrowful individuals succumb to hopelessness, thinking that because they cannot satisfy the most fundamental need in their hearts, they will not attain it. Such is the despairing sadness of the kingdom where those who flee from love live.

Naturally, these two kingdoms have their respective sovereigns. Those who live in the Kingdom of Heaven know that their ruler is God. Those who live in Hell, disturbingly, are not sure who reigns. They think it is they themselves. What is hidden from them is that their sadness, despair, and futile attempts to find joy actually originate from a devilish ruler. This demon, hidden in plain sight and known as the noonday devil or *acedia*, casts a cloud of sadness over reality and so deludes his citizens into thinking that life is not good. If we want to be free of this tyrant's deceits, it is absolutely necessary to expose him to the light of truth.

Acedia: Spiritual Sadness

First and foremost, *acedia* brings about a particular form of sadness, namely sadness at the spiritual good of man. But like any form of sadness, it is an affective response to something that we find distasteful. Imagine the 10-year-old boy who is eating dinner with his family. He joyfully eats his chicken nuggets and expectantly awaits the coming dessert. But his mom tells him that first he has to eat his broccoli. The boy's countenance changes instantly. He looks down at his plate mournfully. He moves his broccoli around his plate, delaying the inevitable. Dinner had been going so well! And now this!

What is happening here? The boy, whose body is disposed towards chicken nuggets, naturally sees in them something befitting his nature. This fittingness brings a certain joy to him as he contemplates eating. However, in the face of broccoli, he experiences sadness because he sees in them something inimical to him (or at least unseemly). Who knows what this

Chapter 1: Naming the Darkness

food could do to him?! This sadness stunts his activity. Whereas joy moved him to eat, his sadness moves him away from eating. Consequently, he aimlessly moves his broccoli around his plate. He is acting, but his actions have no meaning, no purpose.

Sadness, then, is the heart's response to the possibility of uniting ourselves to something that we perceive to be unfitting to who we are. It discourages us to act toward that union. Hence the reluctance to go to that holiday party at the house of a difficult relative. Union with that person seems ill-suited to who one is. So we avoid the activity that causes sadness.

Of course, as we see in the case of the boy, sadness does encourage a certain type of activity: that of distraction. The boy moves, not towards eating the broccoli, but in the hope that he can distract himself until the cause of sadness goes away. Likewise, someone may write many E-mails simply to avoid responding to the one about the holiday party. I once had a housemate whose bedroom was a disaster except when he had papers to write. Then cleaning his room suddenly seemed much more appealing. So in one way sadness discourages activity; in another way it promotes it.

Now as regards *acedia*, we are dealing with a particular type of sadness. According to St. Thomas Aquinas, *acedia* is a sadness that arises from the possibility of friendship with the transcendent beauty which is God.[8] We glimpse, in visible form, the glory of God, and we long to be united to it, to be a part of that beauty. We want to become friends with the Source of all goodness, such that when people look at us, they see a resemblance with the glory of heaven. By *acedia*, however, such a possibility awakens not joyful hope, but despairing sadness.

Of course, we have to ask, why would friendship with God be a source of sadness? Why would someone look at union with God and think that it is ill-suited to his nature? This can happen for two reasons. First, quite simply, because being a friend of God is difficult. "A friend is another self," as Aristotle

---

[8] Cf. Thomas Aquinas, *Summa Theologiae,* Latin text edited and translated by Laurence Shapcote (Lander, Wyoming: Aquinas Institute for the Study of Sacred Doctrine, 2012), II-II, 35, 2. Much of what follows draws from St. Thomas' articulation of *acedia* and its effects on the soul.

says.[9] Friends share each other's hopes and desires. They rejoice and grieve over the same things. Friends become like each other. Friendship with God is no different. To be united to the beauty that we behold means nothing less than to be transformed into it. And that, we realize, demands a real conversion. After beholding the beauty of God for a moment, we come back down to earth and realize that we fall far short of that glory. We had the illusion of belonging to that world. Now we return and find that it was not so.[10] We are still immersed in drudgery and futility. How can I, in my state, look like *that*?

We see here how important it is that the Christian draw his hope not from human power but from the will of God who desires to unite us to Himself. No amount of human effort will ever transform us enough to radiate God's glory. It is not by focusing

---

[9] Aristotle, *Aristotle's Nicomachean Ethics*, trans. Robert C. Bartlett and Susan D. Collins (Chicago: The University of Chicago Press, 2011), IX, 4.

[10] Cf. C.S. Lewis, "The Weight of Glory," in *The Weight of Glory and Other Addresses* (New York: Harper Collins, 2001), 30.

on our transformation, but by focusing on relationship with God that we are transformed. Our conversion flows forth naturally as a fruit of union with Him. If we fail to look at God who has chosen to make us His friends, we will certainly be saddened by the possibility of friendship with Him because it will simply look too difficult to attain.

The second reason we may find friendship with God to be dissonant with our nature is because of the need for the humble acceptance of divine aid. We have such a strong longing for happiness and fulfillment that we fear to entrust our beatitude to another. Our happiness, so we think, will be more secure if it is something dependent on us, on what we can accomplish by our own power and is under our control. We do not want to rely on another for fulfillment.

The problem is that becoming like God means just that. In Him, we find that fullness of life is experienced in a communion of love. What we most need in life, our true nourishment, is not something that we can attain by our own efforts because communion

Chapter 1: Naming the Darkness

demands that we freely give ourselves.[11] Fulfillment comes as a gift or it does not come at all. The one who stubbornly refuses to let go of his life, fearfully grasping on to the happiness he can attain by himself, will never know the supreme beatitude that comes from love, human or divine. And so we find that someone can be saddened by friendship with God out of a refusal to accept anything as a gift. Such a person will not want to share a life with Someone whose activity consists in such self-forgetting love.

This flight from the promise of transforming love, then, is the unique form of sadness that is *acedia*. And like any form of sadness, it results in a flight from what causes sadness. But there is something troubling about *acedia*. Unlike sadness because of broccoli, which only stunts the activity of eating broccoli, *acedia* brings sadness to someone because of who he fundamentally is. To be human means to be created for union with and transformation in God. The one who is saddened by friendship with God

---

[11] Cf. Joseph Ratzinger, *Eschatology: Death and Eternal Life* (Washington, D.C.: The Catholic University of America Press, 1988), 96.

does not lose the will to do one particular activity; he loses the will to be human at all. In the final analysis, *acedia* is man's joyless flight from self, wishing that he had been made for a less dignified fulfillment, wishing that God had not created him to participate in His own nature, but had instead left him alone.

The consequence of this sorrowful flight is devastating. "In order to have joy in anything, one must approve of everything."[12] So we find in Nietzsche. His words do not suggest some facile approval, but a fundamental stance towards reality. How often do we experience some moment of delight only to find it slipping away because of a fear that it is only an oasis in the desert of reality? What is really real is not joy, but brokenness and misery. Nietzsche's genius reveals that we can only experience genuine joy if we believe that the foundation of the world is love, that the world is in harmony and that creation is directed

---

[12] Friedrich Nietzsche, quoted in Josef Pieper, *In Tune with the World: A Theory of Festivity*, trans. Richard and Clara Winston (South Bend, IN: St. Augustine's Press, 1999), 25-26.

Chapter 1: Naming the Darkness

towards fulfillment. The fundamental condition for joy is a universal affirmation of creation.

The man afflicted by *acedia*, however, who is saddened by his existence, cannot make this act of affirmation. He sees the gift-nature of reality. He sees that self-forgetting love is the origin and destiny of creation. But he does not see *himself* as being in harmony with what he sees. It does not appear to him to be good, to be suitable to his nature. Consequently, he cannot give the approval that makes joy possible. Nor, for that matter, can he experience the cathartic sadness that comes to someone who mourns over the loss of a surpassing good. Living without love, he neither experiences joy nor tragedy, but only that indifference so characteristic of our age. Such is the devastation wrought by the noonday devil as he attacks modern man.

A Change of Vision

From this sadness, a change comes over the person's vision of the world. Our loves affect how and what we see. If someone asks my father what he sees when he looks at my mother, he will give a short laugh, smile, and then stammer as he hopelessly looks for words to describe her. How could he possibly put the mystery that is his wife into words that would adequately communicate what he beholds? Impossible. This is what love does to someone's vision. What he beholds is not just an object for research or a commodity that can be expressed by measurable facts. No, he beholds the mystery of a person, the full expression of which can best be articulated by silence. Love expands one's vision to see the mystery of reality.

The person wholly overcome by *acedia*'s influence, however, who loves nothing and no one, loses the capacity to see more than what can be empirically verified. Everything appears to him to be distant information rather than something so close to him that he can no longer see it clearly. In some ways, there is more certitude in what he sees. Everything can be weighed and measured. But that certitude gives him less, not more, access to reality. It is worth keeping this in mind, given our hubris in making everything we experience accessible by the use of digital code. As much information as our devices may communicate, if they do not foster love for what we are seeing, they will actually damage our ability to experience reality. Our eyes do not see as well when they are void of love.

Acedia's Offspring

At this point, we are now able to consider what life looks like in *acedia*'s Kingdom. When this spiritual sadness reigns over someone's life, what type of person does he become? What sorts of activities busy someone who is blind to the divine beauty all around him and who flees from his transcendent destiny? The answer is found in what are called the "daughters" of *acedia*. According to Christian tradition, *acedia* is numbered among the seven capital sins. That is, it is one of those sins that naturally give birth to other sins (hence, *acedia*'s "daughters"). The reason for *acedia*'s presence among these capital sins is simple. We do not like being sad. And so we try to avoid whatever causes sadness. From this avoidance comes other vices that give shape to the life of someone living under *acedia*'s rule.

Despair

The first vice to spring forth from *acedia* is despair. Ultimately, despair is recognizing that one's goal is impossible to attain. The person living in *acedia*'s world sees that union with God is the goal of his life. He recognizes the beauty of divine love in Jesus Christ, but he is saddened by it (or apathetic to it). Thus saddened, he does not think it is possible for him to attain the fullness of life. The boy saddened by the broccoli does not think he is capable of eating such food. Likewise, the one who thinks that God is unsuitable to his nature will not think that he can achieve union with Him.

This despair is closely related to anxiety, as we see even on the natural level. Although depression differs from despair, inasmuch as the latter is a willed decision against a supernatural good, we can gain insights into despair's effects by looking at its natural analog. The depressed person has lost sight of his goal in life. And this loss of purpose brings anxiety. When someone has a goal, he may have many different activities that he is engaged in, but they all make sense when they are seen in the light of that one goal.

Chapter 1: Naming the Darkness

For example, a person who sets out to make a cake looks at the many different ingredients and knows how they all fit together. There are many different foods, but they all make sense. Without the goal of making a cake, however, the ingredients become a source of anxiety. What do I do with all of this? There appear to be way too many things now, and none of them seems to fit in with the others. Without "cake," the combination of flour, eggs, and sugar does not seem to make a whole lot of sense.

This is what happens to the person who despairs. He has lost sight of his goal in life. And without this goal, he does not know what to do with his many different desires. He wants to spend time with friends, to accomplish some great task, to have fun. But all for what? There is nothing that unites his activities. And so his life becomes a source of stress for him.

This, then, is *acedia*'s first-born child. Being saddened by his own existence, the man in *acedia*'s Kingdom despairs of finding fulfillment and lives in a state of stress. Together with despair, the man in this condition becomes incapable of suffering difficulties in pursuit of the good. A person who thinks that he can attain some goal will not become discouraged when difficulties come his way. Indeed, he may even find joy in them. I have heard, though this baffles me, that some people actually enjoy running in the rain (or running at all). They delight in the discomfort they suffer for the sake of their goal. But if someone has despaired of attaining his goal, discomforts become sources of complaints. We think here of the person who leaves his coffee mug in the office sink because he cannot be bothered to clean up after himself. Likewise, we have in mind the person who will not confront an erring superior because it is just too much of a hassle and a risk. A sibling of despair, this complaining and timid spirit belongs to those living in *acedia*'s Kingdom.

Flight from Beauty

The next defining characteristic is a disgust for beauty. When a garden is teeming with life, the dead tree stands out all the more visibly. But if everything in the garden is dead, who notices the tree? Likewise, in the presence of spiritual beauty, of a person whose life radiates divine love, the person in flight from that beauty notices his inadequacies more painfully. He

Chapter 1: Naming the Darkness

hates that someone or something should remind him of the life he is fleeing. He scorns anything that might recall that reality is, ultimately, a gratuitous gift. He wants, instead, to make everything else ugly so that he can blend in to his surroundings.

In our day, we seem to find this in a repugnance towards the sacred, towards visible expressions of being wholly set apart for God. People try to weaken the witness of the celibate priesthood. We are told that consecrated religious should "blend in" with everyone else. More and more couples desire to have their wedding outside of churches, in secular venues or outdoors. In all of this, there is a resistance to the sacred. We want everything to belong to the sphere of the workaday world, to the everyday and commonplace aspects of our life. Not that there is anything wrong with that sphere! It is where we spend the majority of our lives. But the sacred is that which is clearly and visibly set apart for God and so serves as a reminder to us of our destiny. The person who grieves over his transcendent destiny, however, does not want to be reminded of his goal. Consequently, he despises the sacred. He wants everything to belong to the sphere of the profane so that he can remain comfortable in his complacency.

Of course, it is worth asking whether reality is, in fact, beautiful. Does beauty reveal reality, or does it merely distract us from the true face of the world, being an opiate for the masses to prevent social change? This charge cannot be taken lightly. The world is clearly broken. Disney's happy endings are quaint, but they are ultimately dissatisfying. We know that the world does not look like that. Perhaps it is the ugly that reveals reality's true face.

If what is beautiful is true, there must be more to it than the banal charm of fantasy. At this point, we have to anticipate something that we will consider in more depth later on. If it is Jesus Christ who fully reveals the beauty of creation, then we cannot remove the reality of the Cross from that beauty. What makes Jesus Christ shine forth in splendor is not the attractiveness of a model, but of someone whose love is able to dignify even the pain of suffering. How beautiful is the fidelity of a husband to his wife after she has lost her physical beauty. How beautiful is the care of a mother for her son who has a life-long debilitating disease. Indeed, it is precisely by her suffering

Chapter 1: Naming the Darkness

that we come to see how good her son's life is. This is the beauty that reveals the true face of the world. Reality is beautiful not because it is void of suffering, but because the foundation of the world is a love that transforms suffering into something beautiful.

But this is precisely the beauty that citizens of *acedia*'s kingdom detest. Saddened by their true identity, they want to rid themselves of whatever would remind them of the sacrificial beauty of Christ. Underneath the seeming "courage" to expose the ugliness of the world, there is really a despairing flight from the beauty of sanctity. Perhaps no one has better articulated the cynicism of those who flee from sacrificial beauty than President Theodore Roosevelt in his famed "man in the arena":

> It is not the critic who counts; not the man who points out how the strong man stumbles, or where the doer of deeds could have done them better. The credit belongs to the man who is actually in the arena, whose face is marred by dust and sweat and blood; who strives valiantly; who errs, who comes short again and again, because there is no effort

without error and shortcoming; but who does actually strive to do the deeds; who knows great enthusiasms, the great devotions; who spends himself in a worthy cause; who at the best knows in the end the triumph of high achievement, and who at the worst, if he fails, at least fails while daring greatly, so that his place shall never be with those cold and timid souls who know neither victory nor defeat.

"Those cold and timid souls" - such are the souls of those whose lives are governed by the sadness of *acedia*.

Distraction

Finally, the last of *acedia*'s offspring is a spirit of distraction, a certain unrest and wandering of the mind towards artificial and harmful pleasures. Man cannot live without joy. This is why the man living in *acedia*'s kingdom anxiously pursues pleasures. Admittedly, he does not think that they will bring him fulfillment. But what matter? At least they can give him a diversion from the sadness he feels for having fled from the joy he sees in Christ's life. A lustful man pursues sexual pleasure out of a good but distorted sense that it will bring him happiness. Someone afflicted by *acedia*, however, will pursue sexual (and other) delights not because he thinks they will fulfill him, but because he is bored and sexual enjoyment is an easy source of distracting pleasures.[13]

This wandering unrest can manifest itself in mental activity, in speech, and in bodily movements. We see, for example, someone mindlessly "surfing" the web. He is not really interested in studying something needful. Rather, he wants to keep his mind from remembering the reason for his unhappiness: his inability to live with himself. Or again, there is the person incapable of being quiet. It does not matter if he has anything to say, as long as he is saying something. Anything to keep him from recognizing the lack of meaning in his life. Finally, someone becomes incapable of sitting still or of remaining stable in his commitments. Someone who has lost direction in his

---

[13] Cf. Reinhard Hütter, "Pornography and Acedia," *First Things* 222 (2012): 47.

life wants to feel like he is moving *somewhere*, even if it is not towards anything real.

What is troubling about this spirit is that the person so imprisoned by *acedia*'s sadness may not look particularly sad at all. He may well be the life of the party. But behind his energetic conversation, his upbeat movements, and his stimulated mind lies the emptiness of a life that has lost its purpose. In its more subtle form, this spirit presents itself in the inability not to work. The person may be extremely responsible. He may be diligent and industrious. But he has forgotten how to be a friend. He cannot let go and "waste time" with another, simply desiring to know the other's mind and heart. His time with someone must be planned and have a clear purpose.

This can happen even in a person's time of prayer. How often do we go to prayer to figure something out! We wonder how to handle a situation or how to improve our moral lives. These things are no doubt indispensable. But can we imagine a human relationship lasting long if most of the time people spend together is devoted to merely utilitarian purposes? Such a relationship would only last as long as the utilitarian purpose lasted. So, too, in our relation-

Chapter 1: Naming the Darkness

ship with God. If we forget that the goal of prayer is not self-perfection but union with the heart of Jesus, we may well suspect that a workaholic spirit is attempting to drag us down into a hellish existence. All this is to say that *acedia* may disguise itself behind religious language and practices.

In all of this, in the pursuit of pleasure and the inability to escape a worker's spirit even in our relationship with God and others, we see expressions of *acedia*'s last child. The person, despairing of fulfillment and frustrated by beauty, eventually finds that he can no longer rest in anything. He may well be lazy, but no one would call him restful. He lacks that peace of mind so characteristic of the one who has accepted the true meaning of his existence.

Thus it is that we see the portrait of a life spent under *acedia*'s tyrannical rule. It does not take much imagination to see what a resemblance it bears to our world. The despair, cynicism, and exaggerated busyness of the modern age has its origin in the sorrowful indifference of *acedia*. The unifying element in all these characteristics is a flight from the ultimate goal of all human life: union with divine love.

Conclusion

"It is a fearful thing to fall into the hands of the living God."[14] So we read in the Letter to the Hebrews. We are comfortable believing in a God who remains at a healthy distance from us, whose beauty can delight us without inviting us to become like it. But to find ourselves *in God's hands*? To be so close to Him as to be touched and changed by Him? That is far from comfortable. In Jesus Christ, humanity leaves behind the convenience of a complacent life and stretches forward to become one with God's beauty.

This is the adventure that *acedia* attempts to thwart. Satan has no fear of busy workers. Nor of the faux-courage of the cynic. No, such souls do not even merit the attention of his palate. But friends of God? Men and women who are constantly drawn upwards as they live in hope of becoming one with divine beauty? Those are the souls he most fears. In the face of a growing Nazi threat to his beloved homeland, Josef Pieper wrote that,

---

[14] Heb 10:31.

Chapter 1: Naming the Darkness

> Whenever a "new generation" takes up the attack against the resisting forces of evil or against a tense obsession with a security which clings to the delusion that the disharmony of the world is fundamentally curable by cautious and correct "tactics," it is above all necessary to maintain a lively and vigilant awareness that such fighting can only reach beyond sound and fury if it draws its strongest forces from the fortitude of the mystical life, which dares to submit unconditionally to the governance of God.[15]

Does this not beautifully articulate the Blessed Virgin Mary's heart, wholly consumed by Divine Indwelling? Satan will stop at nothing to prevent such magnanimous souls from existing. Through *acedia*, he stealthily imprisons the people of our generation in his kingdom without their even realizing it. And to

---

[15] Josef Pieper, *The Four Cardinal Virtues* (Notre Dame, Indiana: University of Notre Dame Press, 2007), 140.

aid him, he uses the most commonplace (and so invisible) device of all: our screens.

Chapter 2

Digital Seduction

In 1797, Johann Wolfgang von Goethe wrote *The Sorcerer's Apprentice*, a poem about a novice magician whose spells are less manageable than he expects. Wearied by his monotonous task of fetching water, he decides to enchant a broom to do his work for him. Initially, this is a happy success. The broom grows arms, fills buckets with water, and pours it out on the floor. But then the broom keeps going. Soon, the floor is covered in water and the apprentice cannot stop the broom from filling the buckets. He tries to destroy the broom by cutting it in half. But this only serves to produce two brooms doing the work twice as fast. The apprentice realizes that he has no power to stop what he has begun. The broom has a life of its own. Desperate, the novice cries out for the master in words that have become some of the most famous in the German language: "Die ich rief, die Geister, werd ich nur nicht los" (the spirits which I have summoned, I cannot expel). Only the master, the novice discovers, can summon spirits who will remain obedient to him. Anyone else who attempts to do so will find that he is meddling with powers beyond his control.

Over two hundred years after Goethe wrote his poem, Netflix released a documentary, *The Social Dilemma*, which tells a hauntingly similar story. In it, former employees and executives of social media platforms (Google, Facebook, Instagram, Pinterest, etc.) sound the alarm on the damaging effects these sites are having on society. These employees recount the good that they initially hoped to bring about for the world. They wanted to make it easier for people to communicate and to come together by removing the temporal and spatial limitations that make communication slow and difficult. And, obviously, no one can seriously question the benefits of what they have achieved. We can now find information about nearly anything we would want to discover. We can communicate with loved ones across the world without the delay and uncertainty of mail. Aided by technology, the most powerful longing of the human heart, the desire for knowledge and communion, seems to have the secure hope of being fulfilled.

But some of the creators of these technologies are now wondering if they have lost control of what they created. In *The Social Dilemma*, Alex Roetter, a former senior vice president of engineering at Twitter, summarizes the concerns of many: "I always felt like fundamentally [Twitter] was a force for good. I don't know if I feel that way anymore."[16] We are learning again the lesson Goethe taught over 200 years ago: "Die ich rief, die Geister, werd ich nur nicht los." The technology let loose on the world now has a life of its own. And it seems to have gotten out of hand. As we experience more and more the depression, anxiety, and fragmentation of society that these platforms breed, it becomes all too clear: these tools of communication are preventing the very thing they promised to accomplish for us. We do not feel more connected to our world, but less. We are not more unified to others, but estranged. It seems almost like we have summoned spirits to aid us in our task of being

---

[16] Alex Roetter in *The Social Dilemma Trailer*, directed by Jeff Orlowski (Netflix, 2020), 1:07-1:11, https://www.netflix.com/title/81254224.

human and have found that we are no longer in control of them.

Technology and Vulnerability

We have to be careful when we ask technology to help us live more human lives. In a world plunged into disorder by sin, human greatness shows itself in the ability to endure hardships for the sake of what we love. This is why the Cross is so attractive. This is what draws us to the lives of the saints. In them, we see the real potentiality of human existence: to reveal love that endures even unto death. In the face of that which would take everything from them, they refuse to grasp for life. Realizing that life means communion, they prefer to patiently wait for love's gift of self rather than settle for a less beatifying fulfillment.

So when we look to a technology to aid us in making life more human, we have to ask what we mean by that. Does it make us more capable of loving? There is no question that technology makes life more convenient and less painful. But that is not the same thing as making life more human. Indeed, by removing the need to suffer inconvenience and hardships, it may make life less human as we become less disposed to offer ourselves in sacrificial love and less capable of *waiting* for the other to offer himself as a gift.

This is not to condemn technology as evil. Nor is it to encourage a facile rejection of the real benefits of technology. Rather, all this serves to highlight the complexity of our situation. We seem to be a complicated lot, we humans. On the one hand, we want to have control, to remove difficulties and inconveniences from our lives. And, indeed, it would be irresponsible for us to neglect God's gift of intelligence that makes us capable of governing ourselves.

And yet on the other hand, we find ourselves occasionally doing things that are intentionally risky. We jump out of airplanes. We go camping in the woods *where bears live*. We speed down snow-covered mountains with two pieces of wood attached to our feet, reaching speeds of 95 mph, and then when we get to the bottom, we go up and do it again. As much as we want control, we do not seem to want too much of it. We want to feel the inherent danger of living in this world.

C.S. Lewis, in one of his most celebrated passages, sheds light on this riddle of human existence. He says,

> To love at all is to be vulnerable. Love anything, and your heart will certainly be wrung and possibly be broken. If you want to make sure of keeping it intact, you must give your heart to no one, not even to an animal. Wrap it carefully round with hobbies and little luxuries; avoid all entanglements; lock it up safe in the casket or coffin of your selfishness. But in that casket – safe, dark, motionless, airless – it will change. It will not be broken; it will become unbreakable, impenetrable, irredeemable. The alternative to tragedy, or at least to the risk of tragedy, is damnation. The only place outside Heaven where you can be perfectly safe from all the dangers and perturbations of love is Hell.[17]

---

[17] C.S. Lewis, *The Four Loves* (London: Geoffrey Bles Ltd, 1960), 138-139.

As much as we want control, we realize that being in total control imprisons us in Hell, in a world void of the adventure of love. It is love, ultimately, that makes life worth living. We take risks, and sometimes in truly destructive ways, because we want to escape the feeling that we are invincible. We want to experience the possibility of being hurt so that we can remember the possibility of being loved. For all of technology's benefits in expanding our dominion over creation, it can begin to work against our humanity by making us ill-disposed to taking risks, unwilling to be vulnerable, incapable of sacrifice.

Modern technology, in particular, has a unique ability to remove difficulties from our lives.[18] Premodern technology (like a fireplace, for example) certainly gives us greater control over our environment. But these technologies demand that we be engaged in the environment that we are controlling. A

---

[18] In my explanation of technology here, I am pulling from Albert Borgmann's "The Device Paradigm" in *Technology and the Character of Contemporary Life: A Philosophical Inquiry* (Chicago: The University of Chicago Press, 1984), 40-48.

fireplace, for example, gives us greater control by giving us the capacity to heat a room. But it gives us much more than merely heat. Several years ago, I visited Katoomba, Australia, located in the midst of the Blue Mountains. The only source of heat in the hostel where I stayed was a fireplace. So naturally, all the guests in the hostel ate their meals in the room with the fireplace. We got to know one another during our time there. We took turns getting wood and keeping the fire lit, exercising mutual responsibility for the community's well-being. One of the guests brought a guitar with him and so we sang songs in the evening around the fireplace. So yes, the fireplace provided us with heat. But it gave us so much more.

Pre-modern technologies like this give us control, but they do so by also providing us with an occasion for responsibility to our family, to the environment, and to the social world beyond our immediate relations. We can only exercise control by interacting with the world we are controlling. We still feel immersed in the world. Pre-modern technology does not foster domination of the world by force. Rather, it encourages us to make the world more human, creating culture.

Of course, seeking to master a world that we are part of can be a rather difficult and painful endeavor. Although a fireplace provides heat, it demands work. We have to split the wood and carry it to the fireplace. We have to get the fire lit, which can be shockingly difficult. And then there is the ever-present danger of having a fire in the living-room. It is important not to romanticize pre-modern technology. We gain greater control, but we remain vulnerable to the dangers of the world we are controlling.

Modern technology, by contrast, grants us mastery over the environment while removing everything that would make that mastery difficult or dangerous. A central heating system, for example, gives us the same thing we are looking for from a fireplace. It gives us heat. But unlike a fireplace, it demands no fire-making skills, no unpleasant treks outside on a cold day to get wood, and it is far less dangerous. Everything that we would perceive as a burden is removed. All that is left is the heat. We are able to master the world without being susceptible to its dangers. The trade-off, of course, is that we feel less connected to the world we are controlling. We have no idea how our heaters warm our houses. We only know that they do. As modern technology dominates the cultural landscape, we become less vulnerable to the dangers of the world, but also less a part of it. The fruit of modern technology is not culture, but raw power.

Pre-modern technology seemed to strike something of a balance between control and vulnerability, providing a cultural environment that contributed to making life more human. Modern technology, by so effectively eliminating difficulties, may actually have made this task more challenging. It has become easier to gain control, but more difficult to live a fully human life. This is not to say that we have to return to a pre-modern era. But if we want to flourish as a society, we have to soberly examine the challenge that our technological progress has presented to us. We have asked technology to come to our assistance, and it has done so. But it aids us only as it is able. The more we ask of technology, the more convenience – rather than love, which is self-sacrificing and often painful – becomes the standard of human flourishing.

Information Technology: The Joy of Knowing without the Risk

The danger of modern technology in general sheds light on the danger of modern information technology in particular. We have seen that technology augments our natural capacities, giving us greater control over the world and making us less vulnerable to its dangers. Information technology does this for the realm of the mind. Through it, we increase our capacity to know something while, at the same time, needing less direct contact with it, making us less vulnerable to its imposing presence. This is part of our everyday experience. Both the person at a stadium and a person at home in front of his screen can say that he is watching a football game. The person at the stadium does so by the use of his own eyes, the one at home by the use of technology. But both say that they are watching the game.

Of course, the one who watches a football game on a screen has the advantage of avoiding many of the inconveniences that arise from going to the game in person. He does not need to go all the way to the stadium, wait in line, go through security, and then sit in potentially miserable weather. He is able to watch the game without being vulnerable to its environment. The trade-off is that he is not immersed in the world that makes the game more than a series of facts. The miserable weather, the noise of the stadium, all of the "extra" factors that make up the experience, all of these contribute to making the game what it is. The person watching the game on the screen knows *about* these things, but he does not *know* them. In augmenting his power to know the game, technology has diminished intimacy with what he knows.

We can say something similar about our experience of music. Nobody would suggest that the person hearing "Free Bird" live has the same experience as the person hearing a recording of it. The energy of the guitarist feeding off the cheering crowd and the grittiness and imperfections of the singer's voice are part of what makes that song so enjoyable to hear. A recording, with its digital edits and non-existent context, cannot communicate the same reality to the listener. It provides greater access for people to hear the song, for which we should be grateful, but in the process some of the song's depth is lost. The world becomes shallower as it becomes more reachable.

This happens whenever something is made available to us through digital technology. Whether it is a game, a song, a weather report, or another person, whatever we know through this technology loses something of its depth and meaning. There are some things that digital media will never be able to communicate. Obviously, this is not to condemn information technology. Like all modern technologies, it has its benefits and shortcomings. The inner romantic in each of us probably laments that we no longer experience as readily the depth of meaning hidden in reality. But at the same time, it is a great gift for us to have easy access to whatever we want to know. We again confront the paradox of human existence: desire for control and desire to give up control for the sake of intimacy. We want to have reality at our disposal, to be able to unveil every secret. And yet at the same time, we want to know (and not just as an idea) that reality has more depth than we could ever penetrate.

The danger of digital technology, then, is that it will become so adept at representing reality to us and so all-pervasive as our way of encountering the world that we will lose the capacity to confront the mysterious. We will fail to recognize something as more than what can be broken down into digital code and sent electronically to a screen as a perfect representation of the thing itself. We will know the world and others only in a spirit of safety and comfort. Whatever we encounter will no longer make demands of us. We can remain locked in the "casket or coffin of our selfishness" while still experiencing an illusion of joy in knowing the world.

Becoming Like Our Idols

This fear is not just the cry of a romantic who wishes he lived in a pre-digital world. Someone may well object at this point, "Fine. All you've said is probably true. We all experience a certain degree of alienation from the world when we use our devices. But isn't your concern about their destroying our ability to appreciate the mysterious a bit exaggerated? If someone using these devices has a flattened experience of the world, it is his own fault. There's no need to blame the technology for someone using it badly. And, besides, even if someone does have a less intimate encounter with the world and others when he's in front of a screen, why should that affect how he encounters the world when he's not using his device, which is most of his life anyways?"

If only this were so! It is a comforting fantasy to think that the danger is only a matter of *how* we use our devices. We ignore that the very use of them changes our way of knowing something. When people began using forklifts to lift heavy objects, the technology replaced people's muscles. Someone who had never lifted more than a few pounds could now lift piles of wood without any hassle. Obviously, this is a great benefit. But we cannot ignore that the machine now does what the person used to do. And the machine does it *in its own way.*

Perhaps this is too simplistic. The machine does not act autonomously. Humans are still engaged. We may say instead that the person now does with the help of the machine what he used to do using his own muscles. But the effect is the same. The person is forced to act according to the confines of the machine he is using. When using it, he becomes like the machine he is using.

The same is true for digital information technology. The activity we ask them to amplify for us is our capacity to know. And in doing so, we think according to the confines of our devices, which means encountering the world and others safely from the prison of our own minds. Programmers intentionally write algorithms that reflect our desires back to us and we are not even aware of it. When we buy something online, or even search for products, we are presented with other products that *we* may be interested in, given the pattern of our previous buying history. Or when we read an article online, we are offered other articles of the same sort, further entrenching the ideas that we already have inside our minds. To suggest that we are in control here is an illusion. The technology itself is making us ill-disposed to confront something that may pose any threat towards our comfortable lives.

Even more subtly, because anything we see or hear can be turned into digital code and made available to us through our screens, we are not exactly encouraged to leave our comfortable world in order to know something. The football stadium now has to compete with the screen. Anyone who goes to a game in person and experiences the joys it offers certainly knows the benefits of doing so. But it is a very real temptation to think, "Is it really worth it?" Or again, who would go to a happy hour to meet a potential spouse when he can just swipe through photos on an app from the comfort of his home? Again, the point is not that people should only go to a football stadium to watch a game, or that men should only look for women at a bar. The point is that our devices, technology itself, inclines us to act in a certain way. They form a character within us simply by our using them which disposes us to live in a world fixated on ourselves. When we see something through the lens of a screen, we see according to the screen's own limits. It is not a question of *how* we use our technology; our digital devices are not morally neutral.

What is disturbing about this is that our devices influence how we know something even when we are not using them. Their very presence is enough to affect us. Nicholas Carr (one of the leading authors looking at our use of the Internet) told of one experiment in which 520 undergraduate students were divided into three different groups and were asked to take two relatively simple standardized tests. He explained:

> One test gauged "available cognitive capacity," a measure of how fully a person's mind can focus on a particular task. The second assessed "fluid intelligence," a person's ability to interpret and solve an unfamiliar problem. The only variable in the experiment was the location of the subjects' smartphones. Some of the students were asked to place their phones in front of them on their desks; others were told to stow their phones in their pockets or handbags; still others were required to leave their phones in a different room.
>
> The results were striking. In both tests, the subjects whose phones were in view posted the worst scores, while those who left their phones in a different room did the best. The students who kept their phones in their pockets or bags came out in the middle. As the phone's proximity increased, brainpower decreased.

> In subsequent interviews, nearly all the participants said that their phones hadn't been a distraction—that they hadn't even thought about the devices during the experiment. They remained oblivious even as the phones disrupted their focus and thinking.[19]

Once more we see the illusion exposed: our devices do not merely affect us when we are using them. The more they become portable and the more tasks we ask them to amplify for us, the more they will frame our world simply by their proximity.

And even when these devices are away from us, it takes time for our perception to return to its pre-digital state. As we use any technology, our brains change to accommodate themselves to it. This allows us to use the technology with greater fluency. But as new neural pathways form, they weaken and replace old pathways that were formed by activities we no

---

[19] Nicholas Carr, "How Smartphones Hijack Our Minds," *Wall Street Journal*, The Saturday Essay, October 6, 2017, https://www.wsj.com/articles/how-smartphones-hijack-our-minds-1507307811.

longer do. As we use digital devices more regularly, our brains become digital brains. This happens particularly quickly when we use the Internet since it delivers, according to Carr, "precisely the kind of cognitive and sensory stimuli – repetitive, interactive, addictive – that have been shown to result in strong and rapid alteration in brain circuits and functions."[20] Our online mentality remains even when we are offline.

Which, as it turns out, is not very often. In 2015, the average amount of time spent using screen media among teenagers was nine hours a day.[21] Covid only made this worse. And of course, once we are in front of our screens, we cannot simply walk away. Pro-

---

[20] Nicholas Carr, *The Shallows: How the Internet Is Changing the Way We Think, Read and Remember* (London: Atlantic Books, 2010), 27.

[21] Michael Rich, Michael Tsappis, and Jill R. Kavanaugh, "Problematic Interactive Media Use among Children and Adolescents: Addiction, Compulsion, or Syndrome?" in *Internet Addiction in Children and Adolescents: Risk Factors, Assessment, and Treatment*, ed. Kimberly S. Young and Cristiano Nabuco de Abreu (New York: Springer Publishing Co., 2017), 4.

grammers have intentionally made them addictive, offering instant feedback, cliffhangers, the promise of social interaction, and other addictive qualities that keep us in front of our screens.

The problem in all of this is not that digital devices have their own way of communicating reality to us which flattens the world by making it more accessible. Nor is it even that they form a character within us that tends to promote the self. There is a time and place for such flattening and even for a certain degree of self-focus. It would be impossible to grow in virtue if we did not look at ourselves to see where we needed growth or if we simply gazed in amazement at our virtuous friend. This flattening and self-focus can serve the greater good of encountering the other and being united to him. The problem, instead, is that our devices are making this flattened way of encountering reality the only way of encountering reality and the self-focused character our only character. We are becoming disposed to find anything apart from the self to be a source of sadness for us.

We should recall here the myth of Narcissus, the Greek hunter whose infatuation with himself led to his death. As Narcissus gazed at his own reflection in the water, he fell in love with the beauty of the one he saw. Despairing of attaining the object of his desire, he lost the will to live and died (either by an overwhelming sadness or suicide, depending on the source). What many forget about this myth, however, is that although Narcissus was consumed with himself, he was not aware of his self-infatuation. He did not realize that the face he saw in the water was his own reflection.

As we ask our digital devices to give us more and more control over our ability to know, we find ourselves in an eerily similar situation to that of Narcissus. Instead of looking at the world and others, we end up fixated on ourselves but do not even realize it. In the 115th Psalm, the psalmist offers a terrifying depiction of those who put their trust in gods of their own making. He sings,

> Their idols are silver and gold,
> the work of human hands.
> They have mouths, but do not speak;
> eyes, but do not see.
> They have ears, but do not hear;
> noses, but do not smell.

Chapter 2: Digital Seduction

> They have hands, but do not feel;
> feet, but do not walk;
> and they do not make a sound in their throat.
> Those who make them are like them;
> so are all who trust in them.[22]

We become like the thing in which we place our trust. When the works of our own hands become our primary aid in living a fully human life, we end up defining "fully human life" according to the confines of those works. Without really knowing how they work, we ask our devices to make reality more and more accessible to us. But in doing so, we are becoming like the screens with which we spend so much of our time: lifeless, rigid, and flat.

And so it is that we find *acedia*'s twisted smile hiding behind the screens of our digital devices. With their constant accessibility and their ability to be used for countless tasks, they have become so integrated into our lives that we no longer think of ourselves apart from them. But that means that we see with their eyes and adopt the character that they promote.

---

[22] Ps 115:4-8.

If this were held in check, they could be of great service. As it is, they enslave us in *acedia*'s kingdom where we sorrowfully avoid those tasks that are genuinely human, demanding transcendence of self by union with God. We become saddened by who we are. Instead, we live in friendship with *acedia*'s daughters, seeking to fly from our true identity and to find joy in amusing distractions.

The Despair of Digital Devices

To recall, the first of *acedia*'s daughters is despair, whose voice tells us that we will not find fulfillment because the task required to do so is too difficult. Of course, the Enemy does not usually articulate his message so clearly since few people would listen to such an obvious loser. Instead, he tells us that pursuing *one thing* is limiting, that we must keep our options open lest we miss out on some better possibility. But this amounts to saying that the pursuit of fulfillment is too difficult. How could one endure the boredom that may come from committing oneself to going to a party before seeing if some better party is available? How can a man marry a woman without "testing out" what it would be like to be with many other women? It is too difficult. The risk is too great. Better to stay safe and keep our options open until we are 100% sure this is right. But because we can never be 100% sure, we remain trapped in a loop of indecision. We despair of finding lasting fulfillment because the difficulty of giving up other sources of joy seems too great.

The Internet amplifies despair's voice. There are, of course, the more obvious expressions of its doing so. In *The Social Dilemma*, Jonathan Haidt points out the connection between social media and depression and anxiety in America's youth:

> There has been a gigantic increase in depression and anxiety for American teenagers which began around... between 2011 and 2013. The number of teenage girls out of 100,000 in this country who were admitted to a hospital every year because they cut themselves or otherwise harmed themselves, that number was pretty stable until around 2010, 2011, and then it begins going way up.

It's up 62 percent for older teen girls. It's up 189 percent for the preteen girls. That's nearly triple. Even more horrifying, we see the same pattern with suicide. The older teen girls, 15 to 19 years old, they're up 70 percent, compared to the first decade of this century. The preteen girls, who have very low rates to begin with, they are up 151 percent. And that pattern points to social media. Gen Z, the kids born after 1996 or so, those kids are the first generation in history that got on social media in middle school.[23]

Thanks to our devices, the voice that says, "you'll never measure up," is being heard loud and clear by our most vulnerable. There is the felt need to appear perfect, to never make a mistake, and to get enough "likes" among peers. It is an impossible task, one that introduces our youth to the spirit of despair and prevents them from experiencing the joy of adventure.

---

[23] Jonathan Haidt in *The Social Dilemma*, directed by Jeff Orlowski (Netflix, 2020), 0:00-1:13, https://youtu.be/Ui0UNXsEGJ8.

They become stuck in a loop of continuous affirmation-seeking, all the while failing to look towards that Face which alone brings lasting assurance.

But perhaps more dangerous is despair's persistent whisper that speaks to us whenever we have our devices around us. Again, the subtle lie of despair is that we cannot commit to one thing because we will be missing out on some more fulfilling thing. We must not live in the present moment. And our devices actually *discourage* us from committing to one thing. If someone goes on Facebook for the sole purpose of finding out a friend's birthday, he is bombarded by other friends and their activities. If someone goes on Amazon to buy toothpaste, he will see what other people who bought that toothpaste bought in addition to that. Every webpage we open offers us links so that we do not feel trapped on one page. And of course, if we are doing nothing at all, we may as well check our phones, just in case.

In other words, distractions are flung at us, training us not to persevere in pursuing one goal or to live in the present. We unreflectively assume that having one device that gives us access to everything is a great benefit. Instead, however, it makes us fearful of being "tied down" to one activity. Consequently, we become depressed and anxious because we do not know which activity to choose. The voice of despair that tells us to keep our options open, that no one thing can bring fulfillment, becomes the soundtrack of our lives.

As we grow accustomed to this voice, we become less capable of suffering inconveniences for the sake of a difficult goal, or really for the sake of any goal. When we are acting for a definite purpose, we are capable of enduring remarkable hardships for the sake of attaining it. But if we lose our purpose by desperately trying to keep our options open, we begin complaining about any little inconvenience. Matthew Crawford explains that a technological world in which everything exists for the sake of the user offers virtual reality as a moral ideal, damaging our ability to deal with uncomfortable contingencies. He explains:

> ... a fully smart technology should be able to *leap in* and anticipate our will, using algorithms that discover the person revealed by previous behavior. The hope seems to be that

> we will incorporate a Handy Dandy machine into our psyches at a basic level, perhaps through some kind of wearable or implantable device, so that the world will adjust itself to our needs automatically and the discomfiting awareness of objects as being independent of the self will never be allowed to arise in the first place.[24]

The digital world is a world of self-focus. We become incapable of dealing with things that make us feel uncomfortable because it suggests that some things may exist for their own good and not solely for ours. We become fragile people who, in Crawford's words, "can't tolerate conflict and frustration."[25] This lack of endurance is so extreme that "average viewers [of online videos] begin to abandon a video if it takes

---

[24] Matthew Crawford, *The World Beyond Your Head: On Becoming and Individual in an Age of Distraction* (New York: Farrar, Straus, and Giroux, 2015), 72-73 [emphasis original].

[25] Ibid., 77.

more than two seconds to buffer…"[26] Once a task becomes the least bit inconvenient, we readily abandon it.

As we live in a digital world, we are trained to adopt the customs of those who live in *acedia*'s kingdom. From our sorrowful flight from self, we despair of finding fulfillment and become lazy and irritable. This, in turn, leads to our adopting the next characteristic of the slothful man: disgust for beauty.

Digital Trivialization

The encounter with beauty has a uniquely ennobling effect upon us. It prevents us from living in complacency by awakening within us a longing for something other than the self. By giving us a desire that is stronger than our desire for self-fulfillment, beauty has the power to draw us out of ourselves. And paradoxically, it is precisely because we cease living for fulfillment that the fullness of life comes to

---

[26] Adam Gazzaley and Larry Rosen, *The Distracted Mind: Ancient Brains in a High-Tech World* (Cambridge: MIT University Press, 2016), 113.

us. Through the encounter with beauty, man is lifted upwards towards his true and lasting home.

In light of this beatifying experience of beauty, it seems hard to imagine that anything could give us a disgust for it. But we are forgetting one of the most painful parts of our experience. The world seemed so dull and then – "whack!" – we are hit with a vision that makes life seem like it is worth living. But then that vision fades. We return to the monotony of our exile. The vision, it seems, was a cheat, along with its promise of fulfillment. Despair whispers gently to us until we begin to hate the vision that we had and the illusion of joy that it brought. "Beauty," we think, "must be just a distraction. Better not to think of it." In our despair, we come to resent the upward call of beauty.

What despair hides from us, of course, is that the fulfillment revealed by beauty can be achieved only by one who is ready for sacrifice. The vision fades not because reality is, in fact, dull, but because we must be transformed by sacrificial love until we become capable of beholding reality without grasping for it. Beauty invites us to embark on a journey of self-emptying until we are able to receive what was offered to us in hope. Beholding the beauty of reality is a difficult good that requires sacrifice. But the person who despairs does not understand sacrifice. He thinks that if a good is withdrawn, it means that it is illusory, not that it is simply difficult to attain.

There are many ways that we can take our vengeance upon our encounter with beauty, but the person who is ensnared by *acedia* through his use of digital devices tends to do so by trivializing it. We make beauty cheap and silence its call to sacrifice. Certainly, the most prominent expression of this trivialization is pornography. With pornography, the beauty of the sexual embrace is publicized to be viewed by people everywhere as a tool of selfish pleasure. By doing so, what is beautiful is made trivial, commonplace, meaningless. It suggests that this act, and the joy and union it brings, can be understood and appreciated by anyone. There is no need for love, commitment, or sacrifice. Indeed, by exploiting the sexual act for the pleasure of the masses, pornography removes the very thing that makes sexual intimacy so beautiful, namely, the revelation of sacrificial love through participation in it.

Although this is certainly an extreme example, it seems that those who make use of pornography (either as viewers or as distributors) are, in a certain sense, doing what the digital mindset invites them to do: to make the encounter with beauty something available to anyone, anywhere, at any time, removing the summons to any sort of personal transformation. Our digital devices exist to make everything available to us, to bring whatever we can experience into our own comfortable world. Almost by definition, they exclude that which makes the contemplation of beauty so beatifying, its power to draw us out of ourselves. Instead, the beauty that is made available by digital means is brought *into* our comfortable lives. It does not set us free, but locks us even further within ourselves.

It is important to mention that this trivialization does not happen simply because there are photos or videos *per se*. A mother does not trivialize her relationship with her children because she has photos of them on her phone. And when she posts photos of them on Instagram, she is obeying her natural desire to share something good with others. The challenge, of course, is that in order for her to really share what she sees with others, she has to invite them into her life. If others want to see what she sees when she looks at her children, they have to become like her. Posting images on Instagram only reveals a small part of the reality. The person has to become a certain type of person in order to see the image correctly.

The problem, then, is that our devices negate the need to be transformed by making beauty perpetually and universally accessible. That is what makes beauty fall prey to trivialization. Our devices encourage us to become impatient and angry when true beauty does not immediately reveal itself. Once again, as our disgust for true beauty grows, we find ourselves becoming like those who live in *acedia*'s kingdom.

Digital Distraction

Despairing of finding fulfillment, fleeing from difficulties, and angered by beauty's transcendent call, the person formed by his digital devices finds himself desperately searching for joy. Natasha Dow Schüll offers a horrifying account of what such a search looks like from the perspective of a gambling addict, named Mollie:

> When I ask Mollie if she is hoping for a big win, she gives a short laugh and a dismissive wave of her hand. "In the beginning there was excitement about winning," she says, "but the more I gambled, the wiser I got about my chances. Wiser, but also weaker, less able to stop. Today when I win — and I do win, from time to time — I just put it back in the machines. The thing people never understand is that *I'm not playing to win.*"
>
> Why, then, does she play? "To keep playing — to stay in that machine zone where nothing else matters."
>
> I ask Mollie to describe the machine zone. She looks out the window at the colorful movement of lights, her fingers playing on the tabletop between us. "It's like being in the eye of a storm, is how I describe it. Your vision is clear on the machine in front of you but the whole world is spinning around you, and you can't really hear anything. You aren't

really there — you're with the machine and that's all you're with."[27]

How many of us, mindlessly scrolling down our newsfeed, can relate? We do not really want to find any new information; we just want to avoid the misery and anxiety of a life that has lost its direction.

This is the distractedness that belongs to those who are saddened by *acedia*'s burdensome lies, communicated through our digital devices. One of the greatest joys of being made for communion is the ability to rest in the presence of those we love. The world may be going crazy, but my loved ones are here. So all is well. But *acedia*, drawing us away from communion out of fear of being vulnerable, has taken this joy away. Our alternative to genuine rest becomes mere "staying in the machine zone" where "you're with the machine... and that's all you're with."

---

[27] Natasha Dow Schüll, *Addiction by Design: Machine Gambling in Las Vegas* (Princeton: Princeton University Press, 2012), 2 [emphasis original].

One might perhaps argue that our devices exist for nothing other than for communion and so actually help us find the joy of "being with" the beloved. The confusion, here, is that people equate communion with connection. Our devices *connect* us, but they do not bring us into communion. For that to happen, we need to be vulnerable. We cannot experience the joy of communion if we deny the possibility of painful separation. The connection our devices offer us, however, remove that painful possibility. On the one hand, we never need to fear separation since we can always connect with our friends. On the other hand, we are never really close enough to our friends that separation would cause us any fear. When our phones are around, there is always an "out" if the conversation becomes too uncomfortable. Ironically, we become isolated even as we connect to more people. This connection allows us to be with others, but it eliminates both the pain and the joy of real communion.

This blurring of the distinction between communion and connection is, in fact, celebrated by the marketers of digital devices. "Cooking Together" is a commercial for Amazon's Echo.[28] In it, a young woman is preparing a meal alongside her dad. She runs around the kitchen as he calmly gives her instructions and shares his own experience of the young woman's mom cooking the same meal for him. As the young woman's dinner guest arrives, she asks her dad, "How do I look?" Only then does the commercial reveal that the dad is not, in fact, in the kitchen but has been giving her instructions over her device. The commercial, as evidenced by its title, suggests that this device can mediate another's presence so effectively that it is as if the other is really there. It offers connection as a alternative to communion.

Depriving us of the joyful rest of "being with" others, our devices instead offer idle distractions as a substitute. Carr argues that this is an intentional design of programmers, following Google's lead:

---

[28] Amazon Echo, "Cooking Together," advertisement, aired December 30, 2019, during Doctor Who on BBC America, 30 sec., https://www.ispot.tv/ad/dmE_/amazon-echo-show-cooking-together.

Chapter 2: Digital Seduction

> Google's profits are tied directly to the velocity of people's information intake. The faster we surf across the Web — the more links we click and pages we view — the more opportunities Google gains to collect information about us and to feed us advertisements. Its advertising system, moreover, is explicitly designed to figure out which messages are most likely to grab our attention and then to place those messages in our field of view…. The last thing the company wants is to encourage leisurely reading or slow, concentrated thought.[29]

The online world is a fast-paced, constantly moving world, to say the least. And it is designed to be so. The average amount of time people spend on one webpage is between 19 and 27 seconds.[30] This is hardly indicative of a restful heart that is at peace where it is.

---

[29] Carr, *The Shallows*, 156-157.

[30] Ibid., 136.

Furthermore, nobody actually reads what is on a webpage. They scan. Researchers used eye tracking scanners to determine how users read webpages. What they found is that people tend to look at the top line of the page, then the left-hand column, then a little of the middle of the page, and then back down the left-hand column. This is why programmers put the most important content at the top, in the middle, or down the left side of the page. They want to grab our attention and keep us clicking on more links. Our capacity to simply rest with others, or to slowly savor reality, is being taken away from us and sold to the highest bidder.

In short, we are encouraged to "rest" by mere wasting time. What a miserable alternative to the time we "waste" with our loved ones. The digital mindset, having stripped us of our capacity to find meaning in our life through communion with God and others, offers us the poor substitute of distraction. And so it is that our use of digital devices imprisons us in *acedia*'s kingdom, making us more and more like its citizens who are known for their despairing sadness and inability to suffer, for their desire to remove any real beauty from their lives, and for their constant state of distractedness.

Before bringing this chapter to a close, I cannot keep from sharing the quote that awakened me to my own imprisonment within *acedia*'s kingdom. We all know that life with our devices can become a bit dull. But we are not often aware of our real danger, that we are losing the capacity to live with ourselves, to be at peace with who we truly are. In his characteristic clarity, the philosopher Josef Pieper wrote in 1939,

> The degeneration into *curiositas* [the distracted unrest of the mind] of the natural wish to see may be much more than a harmless confusion on the surface of the human being. It may be the sign of complete rootlessness. It may mean that man has lost his capacity for living with himself; that, in flight from himself, nauseated and bored by the void of an interior life gutted by despair, he is seeking with selfish anxiety and on a thousand futile paths that which is given only to the noble stillness of a heart held ready for

sacrifice and thus in possession of itself, namely, the fullness of being.[31]

Paradoxical as it may seem, it may well be the person who "misses out" on all the online affairs who alone avoids missing out on the one thing that matters: beholding the beauty of God's Face.

Conclusion

Admittedly, this chapter has been rather tough on technology. It is probably worth recalling the good that we initially hoped technology would bring about for us. Life is hard and dangerous, and we need aids to make us more capable of living in such a threatening environment. Thanks to technology, those living in North Dakota's harsh winters are able to do more than merely try to survive. Thanks to technology, people can still expect to eat and drink even when there is a drought in their region. Without

---

[31] Josef Pieper, "Temperance" in *The Four Cardinal Virtues*, trans. Daniel F. Coogan (South Bend: Notre Dame Press, 2007), 201.

these aids, we can hardly imagine living a fully human life.

But at some point, technology hinders rather than aids our ability to find fulfillment. Human life flourishes not when we remove all difficulties but when love is allowed to show itself in suffering. If our technologies hinder our capacity for love by turning us exclusively inward, we will find ourselves incapable of joy and fulfillment. And it seems like we have reached the point where this is happening.

The technological forces now at work in our world have surpassed our capacity to control. Our digital devices have become so much a part of who we are that we cannot think of ourselves apart from them. As we become more and more like them, we find ourselves sorrowful, despairing of finding fulfillment, angered by beauty's summons, and seeking pleasures in distraction. In other words, we become citizens of *acedia*'s kingdom. Our technology is now in the driver's seat and is moving us towards a hellish existence of boredom and isolation.

For many, this is not news. We already knew that our devices were sucking life from us. But what can we do about it? Many have tried various ways of freeing themselves from their devices and have fallen back into a sorrowful existence. What this chapter hopefully revealed is the true enemy at work behind our screens. If we are unaware that it is *acedia* that we must fight, our plans of attack will inevitably fall short. Spiritual sloth, the flight from the greatness of a life lived for God, will continue to sneak its way back into our lives. Only when we confront the spirit behind our devices will we be able to move towards real freedom. The *spiritual* battle is the battle that we must learn to fight. And the Church is uniquely suited to engage in such warfare.

Chapter 3

Light in a Land of Shadows

On Feb. 17, 1941, the Gestapo came to Niepokolanow, the largest monastery in the world at the time with over 700 Franciscan friars. These Nazi police came to this haven of peace to arrest the founder, Fr. Maximillian Kolbe, whose proclamation of the Gospel threatened the Nazi project. Fr. Kolbe peacefully submitted himself to the Gestapo's power, blessing his brethren one last time, saying, "I shall not see you again." Soon, Kolbe found himself in the most heinous concentration camp in existence: Auschwitz.

This "work camp" was designed to strip its inmates of their humanity. At his arrival, Kolbe was stripped, shaved, and tattooed with a number, 16670 – his new identity. It was not long before this new environment began to force its dehumanizing conditions on the tormented prisoners, compelling them to forget their dignity and behave like animals, stealing fellow prisoners' food, fighting, and grasping for anything they could to survive. Others so despaired that they threw themselves against the prison's electric fence.

Into this hell on earth, Fr. Kolbe brought a presence that shook the very foundations on which Auschwitz was built. In a camp designed to make people forget their worth, Kolbe never forgot his for a moment and even restored dignity to his fellow prisoners. When someone would steal his food, he would offer more freely, saying, "You must survive this war. As for me, the Immaculata has a mission for me here."

In late July of 1941, a prisoner escaped from Auschwitz. Accordingly, the prisoners were brought out in ranks and 10 of them were chosen for the starvation bunker. One of the men who had been chosen began to cry out, "My wife! My two children!" Naturally, the guards were unmoved. Likewise, all the other prisoners could only think of their own luck in not being picked. Or rather, all the prisoners but one thought this. Number 16670 stepped out of line and calmly walked to the front where the camp leader was standing. The Nazi guards were paralyzed by shock. No one knew what was happening. Kolbe, meanwhile, walked to the leader and offered to take the

Chapter 3: Light in a Land of Shadows

place of the man who had cried out. The leader, visibly unnerved, asked who this Polish pig was. Kolbe responded, "A Catholic priest." The exchange was made, and this Catholic priest joined the other nine men in the starvation bunker.

Even there, the dignifying presence he brought could not be wholly extinguished. Usually, horrible noises would emerge from the cells of the starving men as hunger further dehumanized the prisoners. Instead, while Kolbe was there, those who heard the sound coming from the cells thought that they were hearing sounds from a church. Fr. Kolbe led the condemned men in saying prayers and singing hymns to the very end. Even the Nazis were amazed. Finally, Kolbe completed the mission that the Immaculata had given him, bringing Jesus Christ to the Hell of Auschwitz by his death.

"A Catholic priest" was Kolbe's response to the camp leader's question of who he was. In his dehumanizing environment, he did not forget who he was even for a moment. And his sacrifice has transformed the memory of one of the most heinous atrocities of history. Auschwitz will always remain the place where millions of (mostly Jewish) men, women, and children were demeaned, tortured, and murdered. But it will also forever be the place where the true potentiality of human love was revealed. Kolbe's presence transformed Auschwitz into Calvary.

Hopefully, none will ever again experience the dehumanizing conditions of Auschwitz. But threats against the dignity of human life remain and, indeed, abound. We ourselves live in a world designed to make us forget the transcendental worth of human life. We surround ourselves with devices that drown out the voice from Heaven that cries out, "You are my beloved. In you I am well pleased." Incapable of hearing the Father's praise, we look for our value from "likes" and "followers." We distract ourselves from our inner emptiness with amusement. We work and work and work. And slowly, we no longer perceive the beauty of one simple act of love. It is not enough, it seems. Forgetting that the value of human life and activity consists in making God's love present in the world, most of what we do on a daily basis seems to have lost its meaning.

Kolbe redeemed the horrors of Auschwitz by turning his experience into a love story. In the midst

Chapter 3: Light in a Land of Shadows

of the contemporary dehumanizing conditions in which we live, the German philosopher Josef Pieper articulates the Church's ability to effect the same redemption. Referring specifically to the purpose of a church building, he says,

> the more the absolutist claim of what is merely utilitarian threatens to confiscate our entire existence, the more the human being, if he is going to live a genuinely humane life, needs this opportunity to step away occasionally from this tumult of sights and sounds ("buy this, drink that, eat those, amuse yourself here, demonstrate for or against") away from this unremitting experience of being screamed at, and to emerge in a place where silence prevails and thus, real hearing becomes possible, listening to that reality upon which our existence rests and from which it is continually nourished and renewed.[32]

---

[32] Josef Pieper, quoted by Bernard Schumacher in "A Cosmopolitan Hermit: An Introduction to the Philosophy of Josef Pieper" in *A Cosmopolitan Hermit: Modernity*

In a world overshadowed by the presence of our devices, *acedia* removes our everyday affairs from the context of a love story. Our work and our free time have no direction. They become mere noise. In a church, Pieper is arguing, we leave the hustle and bustle of everyday life and enter a realm of silence to hear again the divine love story that is the foundation of our lives. We escape from the noise of the world, not, certainly, to bury our heads in the sand, but rather to remember what the world is all about in the first place. There, the noise is integrated into the melody of divine love and becomes part of the music emanating from the mouth of God.

Acedia creates a world of noise by silencing the melody of divine love. Those imprisoned by this demon have chosen (or have been seduced into) the convenience of self-absorption and cannot get outside of their own heads. The Church, represented in visible form through church buildings, exists to continually re-immerse us in the love story that sets us

---

and Tradition in the Philosophy of Josef Pieper, ed. Bernard Schumacher (Washington, D.C.: The Catholic University of America Press, 2009), 19.

free from our imprisonment. *Acedia*'s despairing apathy has no power over someone who finds meaning in every action of his life because he recognizes it as part of the romance between him and God.

The Church immerses us in this story above all by offering sacrificial worship to God. It is not enough simply to tell the love story between God and humanity, though that, certainly, is indispensable. We cannot possibly contextualize our lives in a story about which we know nothing. But merely hearing the story keeps it at a distance. We may find it moving and beautiful, but it need not affect our lives. By sacrificial worship, however, our lives become immersed in that story. We take time away from work, away from utilitarian profit, and devote it to something that has no useful purpose whatsoever. We take the hard-earned fruit of our toil and offer it on the altar to be burned (at least symbolically).

When this happens, something like a cathartic release takes place. When a husband spends countless hours at his desk to set aside money for some great gift for his wife, he looks back at that time with joy. When he sees his wife's delight at his gesture of love, he looks at those hours and thinks, "It was all worth it." The tension and stress of all his work gives way to joy as he sees, in his wife's eyes, not mere drudgery but the beauty of love. The time and effort were part of a story that made it all meaningful. Of course, this release only happens if his wife finds his offering acceptable. If she does not, the weight of those hours of toil and drudgery is doubled. His ability to see his life as part of a love story depends on the beloved's receiving his gift of self.

This is the liberation that offering sacrifice to God wins for us. All our work, our struggles, our suffering, is offered to God as a gift. And He accepts it in love. This, at any rate, is the theology of the Mass as understood in Catholic teaching, of which even the non-Catholic can be asked to take note. This teaching holds that in the Mass, Jesus joins to his sacrifice on Calvary the infinitely insufficient offerings of love that we present. And through this exchange, our offerings become an object of divine pleasure. At Mass, the believer has the experience of God looking upon the drudgery of his life and smiling upon it as an expression of love for Him. In His eyes, the believer sees his life in an entirely new way. Everything is now filled with meaning.

The gift that the Church has to offer to a world enslaved under the tyranny of *acedia*'s rule is the gift of her being set apart for God in an exceptional way to offer sacrifice to Him. It is the gift of her sacred nature. It is because the Church is set apart from utilitarian pursuits for the purpose of offering worship to God that she is of such benefit to the world. The noonday devil would have us believe that everything belongs to the realm of the profane, to the commercial sphere. Under his dominion, we think that our lives are good only if they are useful, not because they are part of a love story. We are stripped of our humanity as we become mere functionaries. And as we create machines that function better than humans, we wonder if it is really so good to be human at all.

In the midst of these commercial waters, the Church stands as a rock where we can take refuge. She counteracts the universal profanation of *acedia*'s domain by directing her members towards God in sacrificial worship. In her, we transcend the framework of efficiency and productivity and we find value in love. Importantly, the Church does not worship God *so that* we may be free from the utilitarian world, but simply because it is right to do so. The Church does not exist to make us better people, nor to inaugurate social change, but to worship God. The social changes and personal transformation that do come about from the Church's activity are not the goal, but rather the necessary fruit of the Church's directing her members towards God.

By her sacred nature, the Church resists *acedia*'s despairing movement away from relational living. Her entire existence is a *being for* the Other. If *acedia* disposes us to flee from the adventure of a life lived in love so that we can have greater control and security in ourselves, the Church immerses us in that adventure through her sacrificial worship. When our devices shape our daily lives, we see with *acedia*'s eyes and experience only the sadness of toil and drudgery. When sacrificial worship shapes our lives, we see with God's eyes and experience the joy of love. Indeed, by immersing us in the divine love story between God and humanity, the Church's sacred nature is the direct counterattack to *acedia*'s threefold imprisonment in the despairing, profaned, and distracted world formed by our digital use.

The Gates of Hell Shall Not Prevail Against It

Opposed to the despairing non-activity of *acedia*'s citizens, the Church offers the hopeful non-activity of genuine rest. In *acedia*'s kingdom, the laziness of the citizens consists, ultimately, in the despairing thought that fulfillment is not possible. The lazy waste time, but they do not rest. They are at flight from themselves and their humanity, afraid to commit to any one activity lest it hinder them from doing something more profitable. They neither work nor rest because they have lost direction. Their inactivity is a sign of not knowing where they are going in life.

By contrast, the Church's rest is an anticipation of fulfillment. The opposite of work is not inactivity, but *free* activity. On Sunday, she refrains from work so that she can do that for which all her work is done: union with God in contemplation. She does the activity which is the goal of all her other activities. She looks to God to see his Face smiling down upon her efforts of love in this exile. Thus, her rest is in fact a sign of hope of fulfillment. Despite all the proofs that seem to justify despair, the Church is able to "let go" of her tense grasp on her life and simply "be." Her rest is the answer to *acedia*'s despairing laziness.

Second, opposed to the forced and manufactured experience of wonder which is a defining characteristic of our age, the Church contemplatively beholds the grandeur of God's infinity and rests in restless longing. She does not subject nature to an interrogation until she forces the truth out of her, but patiently awaits reality to make herself known. Because she worships the Creator, she has a great reverence towards His creation. She sees the infinite God expressed through the finite. She looks at something as simple as an insect and realizes that this little, annoying critter is so much more than she can possibly comprehend. There is always more to behold. She is drawn, in wonder, to that transcendent Source whose depths can never be plumbed fully by the finite mind.

The Church thus provides the antidote to *acedia*'s digital profanation. When we are online, there is always "more," but that more is deadening. Rather than filling us with the restlessness of longing, we are filled with the restlessness of anxiety. The problem is that our devices do not foster the patient, reverential spirit that contemplative wonder demands. Imprisoned by *acedia*, we do not look for loving union with what we behold since that requires that we get out of ourselves. Instead, our devices manufacture the feeling of "wonder," of having access to more, while simultaneously keeping us locked safely within our heads. By directing us towards God in worship, the Church disposes us to revere creation and so rekindle in us a genuine sense of wonder.

Finally, against *acedia*'s bombardment of perpetual noise and distractions, the Church provides a culture of joyful celebration. In *acedia*'s kingdom, the citizens have been blinded to the goodness of their lives. They can find no reason to celebrate and, instead, distract themselves with amusements, the cheapest and most immediate of which can be found online. These serve only to further tighten *acedia*'s sorrowful hold on them as they forget their inner emptiness and longing for more.

Once again, it is the Church's sacred nature that frees us from this imprisonment. To say that the Church is set apart for worship is nothing other than to say that she exists for festive celebration. Her entire liturgical worship is nothing other than praise for

God and an affirmation of the goodness of all creation. Pieper beautifully explains,

> Christian liturgy is in fact "an unbounded Yea- and Amen-saying." Every prayer closes with the word: Amen, thus it is good, thus shall it be... What is the Alleluia but a cry of jubilation? The heavenly adoration in the Apocalyptic vision is also a single great acclamation, composed of reiterated exclamations of Hail, Praise, Glory, Thanks... Indeed, the Church itself uses the name "thanksgiving" for the sacramental offering which is the source and center of all other acts of worship. The Mass is called and is *eucharistia*. Whatever the specific content of this thanksgiving may be, the "occasion" for which it is performed and which it comports with, is nothing other than the salvation of the world and of life as a whole... Of course, everything depends on whether or not we think the historical world and human life are "made whole" or at any rate "capable of being made whole"

by Christ. This is the all-important question.[33]

This, then, is the Church's answer to the world of digital distractions. Her very existence proclaims an unceasing "yes!" to what God has done. Seeing the salvation wrought in Jesus Christ, she lives in perpetual praise, thereby answering the wailing of *acedia*'s lament that the only joy available to us is that of distraction.

The Church, then, lives in the world much like Fr. Kolbe lived in Auschwitz, as a living antidote to demons of dehumanization. Kolbe managed to live in such a horrific environment and yet never gave in to living according to the conditions of that environment. Likewise, because the Church is sacred, she lives in a world surrounded by devices yet never conforms herself to this age. She lives as an exile in a profane world, looking again and again towards her true homeland. Jesus promised that the gates of Hell

---

[33] Josef Pieper, *In Tune with the World: A Theory of Festivity*, trans. Richard and Clara Winston (South Bend: St. Augustine's Press, 1999), 37-38.

would not stand against the Church. The isolation of this age, fostered by our use of digital devices, cannot stand against the Church as she immerses us in the divine love story between God and the human being through her sacrificial worship.

Living as Strangers in a Strange Land

If the sacred character of the Church is the antidote to the spiritual amnesia thrust upon us by our devices, there are very practical considerations both for the Church and for our use of devices. Before addressing these, however, it is important to articulate the purpose of this book. The goal is not primarily practical. There will not be, for example, "10 habits to practice to avoid enslavement to screens." No doubt, such practical steps are of immense benefit. The goal of this book is not to tell people what to do, but rather to make them think. The hope is to open the reader up to a deeper awareness of reality and so inspire gratitude for what is. Nevertheless, there are some considerations that flow directly from our awareness of what the Church's sacred nature has to offer to a world enslaved by *acedia*.

Chapter 3: Light in a Land of Shadows

As regards the Church, it means that she must engage the digital world not by becoming digital, but by staying true to herself. Certainly, the reason the Church must stay true to herself is *not* because this is beneficial to society, but because she belongs to Jesus Christ. Nonetheless, there is a temptation to think that this belonging to Christ is not enough to attract a new generation, that she will not appeal to the youth if she does not conform to the digital ideals of our day.

Ultimately, this is a question of faith. Do we believe that the human heart is made for God? Do we believe that nothing is more attractive than a life given wholly to God? Anyone who has met a saint knows the inherent beauty of holiness. This does not mean the saint is the one who rejects the world. Quite the opposite! What is so alluring about sanctity is that we see what happens to the profane when it exists for the glory of God. When changing diapers is part of a life lived for God, such a simple act becomes a beautiful expression of divine love. The Church does not need to become like the world to be attractive. Her directing the world towards God adorns the world with grace and beauty.

Sadly, it is often the case in the Church's history that her sacred character is concealed behind a thick fog of worldliness and sin. In our day, we again hear the psalmist's lament:

> Why, oh God, have you cast us off forever?
> Why does your anger blaze at the sheep of your pasture?
> Remember your flock which you claimed long ago,
> the tribe you redeemed to be your own possession,
> this mountain of Sion where you made your dwelling.
> Turn your steps to these places that are utterly ruined!
> The enemy has laid waste the whole of the holy place.
> Your foes have made uproar in the midst
> of your assembly;
> they have set up their emblems as tokens there...
> They have broken down all the carvings;
> they have struck together with hatchet and pickax.
> O God, they have set your holy place on fire;
> they have razed and profaned the abode of your name.[34]

The psalmist painfully mourns the destruction of the Temple's beauty. And the Church does the same. She suffers along with the rest of the world from the ef-

---

[34] Ps 74:1-4, 6-7 (Revised Grail Psalter Translation)

fects of sin. And because she is so beautiful, those effects are even uglier in her than they are in the world.

Again, it is not the purpose of this book to examine the Church's need for reform and renewal. Enough ink has been spilled on that topic recently, not all of which has been helpful. Rather, by examining the great gift that the Church has to offer to a profaned world, it is my hope that she may remember her great beauty and worth and so live in accord with it. What St. Leo the Great said to the individual Christian could be said to the Church at large: "Christian, remember your dignity, and now that you share in God's own nature, do not return by sin to your former base condition."[35] If we recognize what the Church can be for our device-riddled world, we will not want her to be anything other than herself.

As regards our use of devices, they must not be allowed to enter every aspect of our lives. There must be specific times and places that are intentionally

---

[35] Leo the Great, "From a sermon by Saint Leo the Great, pope" in *The Liturgy of the Hours, Vol. I* (New York: Catholic Book Publishing Corp., 1976), 405.

device-free. In general, we do not allow people to play football in a graveyard, not because there is anything wrong with football but because it is sacred ground, not a sports field. Likewise, if a Christian is a temple of the Holy Spirit, he must be allowed times and places in his life where he is disconnected from commercial affairs; and not as something that happens by chance (as it may when someone's phone dies), but intentionally.

Admittedly, this limiting of our devices goes against their very nature and how they are built. But that simply means that the way these devices are designed is inimical to who we are as men and women set apart for God. Thus, the Church poses a challenge to designers that they care more about people than they do about profit. The Church cannot remain silent when she sees her children tethered to the world of practical affairs by tech companies who use every possible means to make their devices addictive and indispensable for everyday living. Such an invasion into every dimension of human life is an affront to the sacred dignity of the human being. Resistance, by means of digital minimalism, is thus an act of self-

Chapter 3: Light in a Land of Shadows

preservation for the person who desires to maintain his humanity.

In addition to setting aside times and places that are device-free, even when we use our devices we must oppose the intended purpose of the designers. Everything about our devices invites us to forget the purpose for which we first reached for them. We meant to check our e-mail, and we found ourselves reading about the latest threats to civilization. We intended to simply text a friend, and we ended up scrolling through our photos. This forgetfulness poses a real existential threat to our understanding of self. We know what a thing is by knowing that for which it exists. "Cutting" gives shape to a knife's existence. Knowing its purpose helps us know what it is. When we accustom ourselves to acting without purpose, we begin to think that our lives have no meaning. Our lives become cheap and superficial since we no longer think they are moving in some definite direction. This is not to say that every moment of our lives must be planned. But we cannot live our lives like a pinball, stumbling from one event to the next, and simultaneously maintain an experiential awareness of our dignity.

When we use our devices, then, it is important that we do so knowing the reason. A prayer before opening our laptops can be helpful. "Oh God, come to my assistance; Lord, make haste to help me." "If your iPhone causes you to sin, pluck it out and throw it away." Anything to force a pause and awaken the will.

Furthermore, we must know our triggers. If going to a news-site inclines someone to forget why he is there and lose track of time, he should avoid that site altogether. Like in St. Benedict's day, the price we must pay for our humanity may be a certain knowledge of worldly affairs. St. Benedict, upon tasting 6th century Rome's threats to his humanity, left the city and embraced an eremitical life. St. Gregory tells us that "when [Benedict] saw many of his fellow students falling headlong into vice, he stepped back from the threshold of the world in which he had just set foot. For he was afraid that if he acquired any of its learning he, too, would later plunge, body and soul, into the dread abyss. In his desire to please God alone, he turned his back on further studies, gave up home and inheritance and resolved to embrace the religious life."[36] St. Gregory then concludes with words that are recited each year on St. Benedict's feast day: "[Benedict] took this step, well aware of his ignorance, yet wise, uneducated though he was."[37] The same supernatural wisdom is required of us. In order to maintain a meaningful existence with our eyes fixed on the place where true gladness is found, we must remove ourselves from any websites that compel us to live without purpose, even if that means less awareness of all that is happening in the world. We will be "aware of [our] ignorance, yet wise, uneducated though [we are]."

St. Gregory the Great articulates this principle beautifully in a homily:

> ...we make use of temporal things, but our hearts are set on what is eternal. Temporal goods help us on our way, but our desire must be for those eternal realities which are our

---

[36] Saint Gregory the Great, *Dialogues*, trans. Odo John Zimmerman, O.S.B. (Washington, D.C.: The Catholic University of America Press, 1983), 55-56.

[37] Ibid.

goal. We should give no more than a side glance at all that happens in the world, but the eyes of our soul are to be focused right ahead; for our whole attention must be fixed on those realities which constitute our goal.[38]

This principle will have to be adapted depending on different states of life. A senator will have to be more attuned to worldly affairs than a priest. But both will benefit from St. Benedict's principle.

Finally, a regular regiment of prayer and meditation must be part of our life. Even more than the ascetical disciplines that serve to limit our use of devices, the positive movement towards remembering the story that we are a part of will serve to keep us free from *acedia*'s chains. St. Augustine said that,

we turn our mind to the task of prayer at appointed hours, since that desire [for eternal

---

[38] Gregory the Great, "From a homily on the Gospels by Saint Gregory the Great, pope" in *The Liturgy of the Hours, Vol. IV* (New York: Catholic Book Publishing Corp., 1976), 1875.

beatitude] grows lukewarm, so to speak, from our involvement in other concerns and occupations. We remind ourselves through the words of prayer to focus our attention on the object of our desire; otherwise, the desire that began to grow lukewarm may grow chill altogether and may be totally extinguished unless it is repeatedly stirred into flame.[39]

By refocusing our attention on God throughout the day at set times, we can resist *acedia*'s voice speaking to us through our devices. The Church's custom of praying the *Angelus* in the morning, noon, and evening, for example, is a great and simple practice. Prayer and meditation serve to keep the eternal homeland for which we long in the forefront of our minds.

I am not intending to give a comprehensive plan of life for people's use of their devices. Such particular advice demands personal prudence and guidance from someone who knows the person involved. But

---

[39] Augustine, "From a letter to Proba by Saint Augustine, bishop" in *The Liturgy of the Hours, Vol. IV*, 412.

each person in our day must examine himself and make some sort of plan for his use of devices. He cannot simply buy them and use them as they are intended to be used. Such a person will soon find his humanity severely damaged as he loses sight of the transcendent purpose of his life.

Creating a New Environment

In the 1970's, the U.S. government faced a serious health crisis. About 20 percent of the soldiers returning from Vietnam were addicted to heroin, and there was no real reason to expect that they would be successful in overcoming their addiction. It is hard enough for an addict to stop using heroin in the first place, and even among those who do, 95 percent of them relapse at least once. The United States was looking at the possibility of hundreds of thousands of soldiers returning home and bringing their heroin addiction with them. The situation seemed dire.

And then the soldiers came home and simply stopped using heroin. It was that easy. In fact, 95 percent of the formerly addicted veterans *never used heroin again*. The statistic was totally reversed. It seemed too good to be true. But the numbers held and experts had to try to make sense of what happened. Before this, the common wisdom placed the blame for addiction either on the substance or on the user. Either some substances are automatically addictive or some users are predisposed towards addiction. But neither of these explanations accounts for the veterans' successful freedom from their addiction. Something else had to be a work.

What the experience of the Vietnam War veterans reveals is that there is something more than merely the product or the person. There is also the environment in which the person uses the product. As psychologists have come to discover, the soldiers' addiction was not a matter of something being wrong with them or of heroin's addictive qualities, but of a war that brought the soldiers to look to heroin as an escape. As Adam Alter explains in his book, *Irresistible: The Rise of Addictive Technologies*, "[Addiction] isn't the body falling in unrequited love with a dangerous drug, but rather the mind learning to associate any substance or behavior with relief from psychological pain."[40] Once the soldiers were taken out of the situation where they experienced horrible psychological pain, they stopped looking to heroin as an escape. Had they returned to Vietnam or been surrounded by a war-like environment, 95 percent of them probably would have relapsed. Instead, without those cues that triggered the memories of the War, 95 percent of them remained clean.

We can learn something from this insight about our use of digital devices. Obviously, not everyone who has a smartphone is addicted to it. But what we know about addiction can shed light on our actions in general and how we use our digital devices in particular. Humans never act in isolation from their context. There is always some context, some situation, that makes the action make sense for the acting person. As the previous chapter showed, our digital devices are creating a new, spiritually apathetic, environment. And within that environment, certain actions and attitudes make sense: despair, flight from

---

[40] Adam Alter, *Irresistible: The Rise of Addictive Technology and the Business of Keeping Us Hooked* (London: Penguin Press, 2017), 90.

Chapter 3: Light in a Land of Shadows

beauty, mental unrest. What is sinister about our devices is that they are like a drug that simultaneously creates an addictive context. Surrounded by our devices, we become saddened by who we are as people who find fulfillment in something we cannot procure for ourselves, namely love. And then, to find relief from our sorrow, we turn to the very thing that saddened us in the first place.

This is why so many fail to find freedom from their smart-devices. We act like heroin addicts who never left the Vietnam War. It is not enough for us to set up restraints. What we need is a new context in which our escapist actions no longer hold any power over us. This is the incredible gift the Church offers the world. By her sacred nature, she provides a new environment of rest, wonder, and celebration that strips the current digital environment of its tyrannical power. Heroin was far less attractive to American soldiers when they were surrounded by loving families and peaceful conditions. Likewise, our devices are far less attractive to us when we are surrounded by realities presented to us by the Church's sacred nature. When we experience our lives in the context of a love story through our participation in sacrificial worship, we are surrounded not by dead things that exist for our convenience, but by living realities whose very existence is a source of wonder and praise.

The challenge is how the Church does, in fact, present such wondrous, living realities to us. We know that it cannot be by merely introducing different things into our lives. How often have we bought a picture because it reminds us of some beautiful event, only to have that picture disappear into the ordinariness of our office within a week of purchasing it? The thing is there, but it loses its power to awaken wonder. Rather, we must become people who are capable of beholding things that have an existence apart from our needs and desires. What needs to change is not so much *what* we behold but *how* we behold. The Church surrounds us with living realities not by changing our surroundings, but by changing us. She makes us a new creation, transforming us into men and women who are *capable of suffering the presence of the other*.

Chapter 4

Divine Conquest

G.K. Chesterton described St. Francis as someone who looked at the world as though he were standing upside down. Standing "right side up," most of us tend to see the world with a certain ambivalence. Things are as we expect them to be. Not much is an occasion of wonder or amazement. I look at a table with books on it and leave it at that. What more need be said? The person standing upside down, by contrast, is amazed by everything. He sees the books, hanging beneath the table, which is itself somehow attached to the floor, and wonders how it does not all fall down. The person standing upside down finds the table and books absolutely fascinating. We, meanwhile, standing right side up, think that the person on his head is rather out of his mind.

But perhaps he is nearer to seeing reality correctly than we are. His inverted vision of the world, says Chesterton, "so much more bright and quaint and arresting, does bear a certain resemblance to the world which a mystic like St. Francis sees every day."[41] The mystic sees creation from the perspective of dependence. For him, all creation is dependent on the Creator for its existence. He is amazed not when things are out of the ordinary or when things go wrong; he is amazed that anything should go right at all. Every breath he takes is a source of wonder for him since that breath would not come but for the will of God. Indeed, for him to cease to exist would require no action on God's part; rather, God would simply have to *cease acting* for him to fall into nothingness. The mystic, so odd to those of us living "right side up," in fact lives far nearer to the truth of things than we.

What is immediately relevant here is the means by which St. Francis (or any other mystic) attained such an inverted vision of the world. What makes it possible for someone to see, not *what* they saw, but *as* they saw? Francis, as many know, found himself in

---

[41] G.K. Chesterton, *St. Francis of Assisi* in *The Collected Works of G.K. Chesterton, Volume II: St. Francis of Assisi, The Everlasting Man, St. Thomas Aquinas* (San Francisco: Ignatius Press, 1986), 70.

something of a dungeon for "stealing" from his father. That is, he sold his father's clothes so that he could collect money to rebuild a fallen church. As it turned out, his father had other plans for that money and demanded full legal justice be done to his son. Such an imprisonment would have come as a humiliation to Francis. He was one of those personalities who liked to be liked. He wanted to be seen as good and upright and honorable. And here he was, publicly embarrassed by his own father and made to be a fool. And in the hole in which he was thrown, he was allowed to sit, meditating on the fact that he was now considered a fool by his own townspeople.

G.K. Chesterton describes the effect of his meditation: "When Francis came forth from his cave of vision, he was wearing the same word, 'fool' as a feather in his cap; as a crest or even a crown. He would go on being a fool; he would become more and more of a fool; he would be the court fool of the King of Paradise."[42] During his time in the cave, Francis learned the truth about himself, that he was nothing. And that truth slowly became the source of an im-

---

[42] Ibid., 72.

penetrable joy. If he was nothing, all was a gift. He would remain nothing all his life, and so be everything. As a jester provided a taste of the joy offered by the King's presence, so St. Francis would be the living embodiment of the joy offered by Christ. Indeed at the end of his life, stripped of all and lying naked beneath the heavens, "the stars which passed above that gaunt and wasted corpse stark upon the rocky floor had for once, in all their shining cycles round the world of labouring humanity, looked down upon a happy man."[43]

This is the universal teaching of the Church's great mystics. St. Catherine of Siena encouraged her disciples to remain in the "cell of self-knowledge" in which they knew their nothingness and God's infinity.[44] More poetically, St. John of the Cross taught his famous "nada" doctrine: "To reach satisfaction in all, desire satisfaction in nothing. To come to possess all, desire the possession of nothing. To arrive at being all, desire to be nothing. To come to the knowledge

---

[43] Ibid., 78.

[44] Cf. Sigrid Undset, *Catherine of Siena* (San Francisco: Ignatius Press, 2009), 40.

of all, desire the knowledge of nothing."[45] Whoever the mystic, the teaching is the same: one goes up only by going down. As someone's dependence on self diminishes and gives way to greater dependence on God, more and more does he see the world with new eyes. He lives in the same world as those who are self-reliant, but sees it differently than they. The one sees dead things, commodities available for his use. The other sees living realities in which he delights for their own sake.

Knowing from Within

One question immediately arises from this consideration: why the need for the experience of dependence? Is it not enough to know by study that everything is dependent on God? Must we also suffer that dependence? Why does experience change our vision in a way that mere study does not? And yet we

---

[45] St. John of the Cross, *The Ascent of Mount Carmel* in *The Collected Works of St. John of the Cross*, trans. Kieran Kavanaugh, O.C.D. and Otilio Rodriguez, O.C.D. (Washington D.C.: ICS Publications, 1991), 150.

know that it is the case. We feel lonely; we tell ourselves again and again that God loves us; and this knowledge does nothing. The loneliness is just as potent as it was before. In fact, it becomes even worse because we experience the extra-added pressure that comes from thinking that we are doing something wrong. Should not the knowledge of God's love change our perception of reality? What, then, is wrong?

The answer can be found in the traditional understanding of types of knowledge. As philosopher Albert Borgmann describes, there is a distinction between knowledge and information.[46] Information is indirect knowledge about something absent. For example, if I want someone to know *about* my sister, there is no need for him to meet her. I can give him information and that is sufficient; she is 35 years old, married, has four children, etc. But no one would suggest that the person who has been given all the information that can be given about my sister, and yet

---

[46] Cf. Albert Borgmann, *Holding on to Reality: The Nature of Information at the Turn of the Millennium* (Chicago: University of Chicago Press, 1999), 14-15.

has never met her, knows my sister as well as I do. There is something indirect about the knowledge that comes only from information.

In traditional terminology, this kind of knowledge is called knowledge *per cognitionem* (scientific knowledge in the strict sense). It is juxtaposed with knowledge *per connaturalitatem* (connatural knowledge). This knowledge comes not from study but from a sharing of natures. St. Thomas Aquinas gives the example of the person who understands the virtue of chastity. On the one hand, someone can know it by study. He may be remarkably lustful and yet be able to articulate the virtue with precision. His "knowledge" of it is of something foreign to him. He knows *about* it, but he does not *know* it. On the other hand, someone may understand chastity by being chaste. He knows this virtue from an inner attunement to and living experience of chastity. He has connatural knowledge of chastity. His knowledge is not the fruit of study but of union with what he knows. It is not of something foreign, but of something intimately united to him.

We experience the same juxtaposition in our knowledge of people. Why is it that some people meet again and again and again and never seem to grow closer, whereas others meet once and experience a real connection after one conversation? The answer is that direct knowledge comes not from exchanging information, but from sharing in the other's nature. The two people get to know each other so quickly because they are like each other. It is as if they had known each other their whole life. One person shares himself with another, and what he shares is able to be received precisely because the two are already alike. Connatural knowledge, direct knowledge of the other, is the fruit of union.

Rather than simplifying things, this distinction between knowledge *per cognitionem* and knowledge *per connaturalitatem* adds a layer of complication to the question of why we must experience dependence in order to know God and to see as He sees. True, it clarifies why mere study of God is insufficient; direct knowledge of God is necessary if we want to see with the eyes of a mystic. But how do we attain this knowledge by the experience of dependence? Surely, nothing could be more *unlike* God than to be dependent. But from what has just been said, we must become *like* Him if we hope to see with His eyes.

Chapter 4: Divine Conquest

Should we not rather flee from the experience of dependence, exalting ourselves to the level of God? How do we become like Him by least resembling Him?

There are two primary experiences through which we become most deeply acquainted with our nothingness: love and death. In both of these experiences, there is a deeply felt sense that our life is not in our hands. The person in love feels keenly that happiness in his life depends wholly on another. He cannot imagine life without his beloved. He becomes intimately associated with his poverty, with his lack of self-sufficiency. Likewise, the person on the verge of death feels life slipping from his hands. He is not in control. He may protest and fight, but he realizes that his life is not, in fact, his. Like love, the experience of suffering and death gives us direct knowledge of our dependency.

But these experiences also make us aware of something that reaches out beyond either of them. The person who has fallen in love longs for something he cannot quite put into words. It is not simply that he wants the beloved. Rather, in loving her, he is desiring something *for* her; but whatever that "for" is, he cannot quite name. "Happiness," "beatitude," "fulfillment," are all attempts to communicate the object of that inexpressible longing that awakens within the heart of one who loves. His love stretches him beyond the confines of his finite mind. Likewise, the person who faces the reality of death is not in a position to name what he fears. That other-worldly repulsion that comes to someone standing before the face of death does not go away by a scientific explanation of the mechanics of bodily termination. He is afraid of something else, for which he can find no name.

The person, then, who becomes acquainted with his poverty through the experience of love or of death becomes acquainted also with his orientation towards the Infinite. Nicholas Cabasilas describes it accordingly:

> When men have a longing so great that it surpasses human nature and eagerly desire and are able to accomplish things beyond human thought, it is the Bridegroom who has smitten them with this longing. It is he who has sent a ray of his beauty into their eyes.

> The greatness of the wound already shows the arrow which has struck home, the longing indicates who has inflicted the wound."[47]

By the enkindling of a longing that surpasses the capacity of human thought to comprehend, our dependence becomes the gateway for union with the divine. We share in God's nature not by making ourselves self-sufficient, but by thirsting for the Infinite, by suffering the wound inflicted by divine beauty. His infinite love meets our infinite longing. We go up only by going down.

If the experience of dependence immerses us in divine life such that we know God through a sharing of nature, our initial understanding of God's self-sufficient happiness becomes highly suspect. The God

---

[47] Nicholas Cabasilas quoted in Joseph Ratzinger, "The Feeling of Things, the Contemplation of Beauty" (message to the Communion and Liberation Meeting at Rimini, August 24-30, 2002), http://www.vatican.va/roman_curia/congregations/cfaith/documents/rc_con_cfaith_doc_20020824_ratzinger-cl-rimini_en.html.

revealed by Jesus Christ is not a solitary Being whose happiness consists in being full of Himself. Rather, divine beatitude consists in being *empty* of self since the Father holds nothing back from the Son, Who Himself has nothing except for what is given Him by the Father. And the Son holds nothing back for Himself but freely offers Himself in the Spirit back to the Father. There is something of a gleeful and reckless abandon in Trinitarian love. This supreme beatitude that exists for all eternity in the Trinity becomes accessible to us through the emptiness of the Incarnation. In Christ, human nature becomes capable of the same joy experienced in Trinitarian love precisely by the Incarnate Word's pouring out of Himself even unto death, death on a cross.

The mystical vision attained by St. Francis, then, was not the fruit of study or of meditation techniques. It sprang from encountering God in the experience of his poverty, which is quite simply the virtue of faith. As he plunged deep into his heart, he recognized an infinite thirst that could not be satiated by anything he could attain by his own power. A Presence was living within him that was not himself. Christ was living His own poverty in Francis, joining

Chapter 4: Divine Conquest

him to the Divine Nature. By faith, Francis allowed God to live the mystery of His Life in him. Accepting his poverty, Francis came to share in the fullness of Life and began to see with God's eyes.

If we wish to see with the eyes of a mystic, we must learn to live in the same poverty of spirit. We do not attain such a vision by meditating on neatly constructed formulas or by perfectly executing our spiritual practices. These are no doubt indispensable aids. But they are the building blocks of faith, not faith itself. They train us to follow something other than our own ideas and desires. But they can become routine sayings or rote practices if they are not enlivened by the virtue of faith whereby we cling to God alone. At some point in our spiritual growth, God Himself steps in and shakes our foundations until we have nothing left but our nothingness and God's Infinity. From this "dark night," we emerge with an unshakeable vision of the world's goodness. We look at creation and say with God, "it is very good." That is, we enter into the Sabbath rest of God. We become surrounded by living realities because we have received new sight through communion with God by faith.

Finding God in our Digital Prison

Throughout the course of this book, I have argued that our digital devices are designed to numb our experience of limitedness. Apart from the obvious distractions that they bring, as a technology they are so efficient and demand so little of our personal engagement that we can accomplish most of our daily tasks without much difficulty. We no longer have to deal with our limitations. They have been overcome by our technology. We satiate our desire at the very moment we feel it. Limitation, desire, thirst – all of these technology has removed from our day-to-day experience.

The result of this is a neutered spirit that can no longer experience joy because it can no longer experience desire. The person, so affected, becomes enslaved in *acedia*'s kingdom. The noonday devil places a sorrowful lens over his eyes and imprisons him in a lonely, profaned, and superficial world. Such has been the devastation wrought by our digital devices.

Of course, the reality is that our limitedness has not been overcome but merely ignored. Our thirst for the Infinite does not go away; it is just buried beneath layers and layers of information which pose as an answer to our thirst. Our desire is still there, but we are sickened by it, like someone with a hangover is sickened by the thought of food. "The Infinite" appears loathsome to us. We do not want more information; we want reality. But to keep ourselves safe "from the dangers and perturbations of love," we have numbed ourselves to reality. How do we solve this dilemma?

I often think about the account in St. John's Gospel of the woman caught in adultery. Who knows what wounds led to her state of depravity? Perhaps a life full of men's lustful glances caused her to forget her true worth and so she sought approval wherever she could find it, no matter how unsatisfying it was. Or perhaps she was simply hardened by injustices committed against women and found this act of adultery as a way of asserting herself over an oppressor. Whatever the case, by the time the Gospel event took place, she was a broken woman. Surely, the family of the man with whom she slept hated her. As much as it was his fault as well as hers, the man's wife and children could not have looked at her without resentment. In addition, the religious leaders, always out to expunge any transgression of the law, saw her as a defilement on their people. They dragged her out to the public square to accuse her.

I imagine by the time she gets there, she is no longer ashamed or even sad. Even her anger against the societal injustice that led to her condemnation rather than the man's has waned. Her psychological defenses come to her aid so that she is not overcome by grief and humiliation. I imagine she is just numb; numb to the accusations of the scribes and pharisees, numb to the hatred of the family, numb even to her own feelings. This whole scene may as well have been happening to someone else. She lays in the dust, apathetic to the accusations hurled against her.

Jesus, seeing this, does not say a word. Notice the *lack* of information that He communicates. He knows she will not listen to more words. He knows that she is not lacking information; she is lacking the *presence of another who is with her* in the hell that she has made for herself to keep her safe. So instead of saying a word, Jesus bends down and begins to write in the dust. And now, all the accusing voices are directed towards Him. Every spirit of guilt, shame, hatred, etc., that afflicted the woman is given a new object of affliction. The woman is no longer at center-stage; Jesus has taken her place. Do we not see the prophesy of the suffering servant already beginning to be fulfilled? "Yet it was our pain that he bore, our sufferings he endured. We thought of him as stricken, struck down by God and afflicted. But he was pierced for our sins, crushed for our iniquity. He bore the punishment that makes us whole, by his wounds we were healed. We had all gone away like sheep, all following our own way; but the Lord laid upon him the guilt of us all."[48] Already, Jesus is taking the sins of others upon Himself.

At some point, the woman looks up and realizes that she is alone with Jesus. Her accusers have left, but something even more powerful than they has remained. Her hell has been invaded. The apathy that long kept her safe from her accusers could not protect her from Jesus. Rather, it is the very place where she finds Him. Jesus is with her. He has become *like her*, providing her with something more than information. For the first time in who knows how long, she is able to live with herself because that self has been loved and affirmed. She is known in her faults

---

[48] Is 53:4-5.

and loved even there. Her heart has become a good place to be.

What is remarkable here is the woman's newfound *capacity to receive* Jesus' love for her. It is the fruit of her own newfound capacity to love another. To receive love, we must give love ourselves. Erasmo Leiva-Merikakis, in his commentary on Matthew's Gospel, rather surprisingly refers to Graham Greene's *The End of the Affair* to articulate this law of love. Sarah Miles, the book's female protagonist, is grappling with love for God, herself, and her illicit lover. In her musings, Sarah recounts her lover's affection for her and her own acceptance of that love:

> All today Maurice has been sweet to me. He tells me often that he has never loved another woman so much. He thinks that by saying it often, he will make me believe it. But I believe it because I love him in exactly the same way. If I stopped loving him, I would cease to believe in his love. If I loved God, then I would believe in his love for me. It's not enough to

need it. We need to love first, and I don't know how. But I need it, how I need it.[49]

Sarah's reflections show us a conflicted heart. On the one hand, she recognizes that she can receive Maurice's love for her because she loves him in like manner. And yet, that very recognition reveals to her the stumbling block she has set up for herself to receive God's love. She will not let God's heart live within her own heart. She will not love like He loves. And so she cannot receive the love He has for her. And yet, Leiva-Merikakis concludes, "these reflections mark an incipient capitulation of her resistance and, consequently, the first glimmerings of her own love for God."[50]

In like manner, the woman caught in adultery only becomes capable of believing in God's love for

---

[49] Graham Greene, *The End of the Affair*, quoted in Erasmo Leiva-Merikakis, *Fire of Mercy, Heart of the Word: Meditations on the Gospel According to Saint Matthew, Volume Three* (San Francisco: Ignatius Press, 2012), 812.

[50] Ibid.

her when, seeing Jesus in her own pitiable condition, she is moved with pity for Him. Being so moved with pity, she becomes interiorly aware of how He looks at her. It is a moment of quiet intimacy, when two hearts become one. Her gaze upon Him is the same as His gaze upon her. From that gaze, feeling floods back into her heart. She can love again. She can grieve again. She can hope again. She has come back to life.

I wonder if this is precisely where we find ourselves. To keep ourselves safe from the experience of our limitedness, we have imprisoned ourselves in a hell of our own making. Like the woman caught in adultery, we do not experience longing for the Infinite because we do not allow ourselves to experience longing for anything at all. And we medicate our spiritual apathy by manufacturing sources of wonder. Or, if we are spiritually aware of our predicament, we try to rekindle a sense of thirst by penitential practices or meditative techniques. Certainly, these have some value. But they can also give way to anxiety and despair as we tensely try to feel something that we think we should be feeling. The assumption is that God cannot be found in our present state of indifference. We think that we have to change ourselves to have a direct encounter with God, the burden falling to us.

Instead, Jesus reveals another way, that of faith. The woman escaped from her hell not by changing herself, but by God's activity within her, giving her the same love that He Himself has for her (Rom 5:5). Her hell simply ceased to exist the moment Jesus entered her heart. Ratzinger describes the effect of the Christ-event:

> The Just One descended into Sheol, to that impure land where no praise of God is ever sounded. In the descent of Jesus, God himself descends into Sheol. At that moment, death ceases to be the God-forsaken land of darkness, a realm of unpitying distance from God. In Christ, God himself entered that realm of death, transforming the space of noncommunication into the place of his own presence.... God has cancelled out and overcome death in entering it through Christ.[51]

---

[51] Joseph Ratzinger, *Eschatology*, 93.

When Jesus came into her life, the woman's state of alienation from self and others simply ceased to be. All that remained was the place of communion with God. Now, whenever she looked at her sad and dreary state, all she would see was Jesus, whose presence with her would draw out love and hope. She did not need to conjure up love out of nowhere, relying on the strength of her own willpower. Rather, she needed nothing more than the faith to see the God who descended to her sorrowful condition. God entrusted Himself and His own poverty to her heart. Trusting His trust in her, she came to recognize the value of her life.

Like this woman, we do not need to *do* more to escape from *acedia*'s kingdom. We need to *trust* more. We need to keep our eyes on Jesus. Wonder is not the fruit of living in a less technological society, but of living with more faith. Living with a grasping, controlling spirit is what imprisoned us in *acedia*'s kingdom because it taught us to rely on ourselves. The only way out is to renounce that spirit and live by faith.

This is precisely what Moses enjoined the Israelites to do as they were on their way from Egypt to the

Promised Land. With the Israelites stalled before the Red Sea, Pharaoh thought he had an opportunity to defeat them and drag them back into slavery. The Israelites were, quite naturally, terrified. In reply, Moses cried out, "Fear not, stand firm, and see the salvation of the Lord, which he will work for you today; for the Egyptians whom you see today, you shall never see again. The Lord will fight for you, and you have only to be still."[52] The Israelites defeated the Egyptians not by any human effort but by standing firm in faith. They let God act and then walked forward through the sea into freedom.

For some reason, by the time God's commandment to "be still" arrives at our ears, what we hear is "do nothing." We assume that trusting God to act amounts to doing nothing, as if God is encouraging us to be lazy. But there is demonic pride behind such a distortion of God's words. In the Septuagint, the Greek word "σχολάζω" (scholazo) is used in only two contexts. One is Psalm 45, in which God enjoins His people to "be still (σχολάσατε) and know that I am God." This psalm is a hymn of remembrance of all

---

[52] Ex 14:13-14.

that God has done for His people and of the power of His love. The Israelites are to rest and look to the Lord who has done such wonderful things for them. It is simply an invitation to renounce self-exaltation and instead to *live in the relationship that brings salvation.*

The only other place in which the Greek term "σχολάζω" is used is in Exodus when Pharaoh reprimands the Israelites for wanting to leave their work so as to offer sacrifice to God. He says, "Lazy! You are lazy! That is why you keep saying, 'let us go and offer sacrifice to the Lord.' Now off to work!"[53] Here, the word "σχολάζω" is now translated as "lazy!" God invites the Israelites to rest and to know His providential care for them. Pharaoh, *using the same word*, says that such rest amounts to laziness. God says one thing and then Pharaoh subtly changes the meaning of what God says and turns it into an accusation.

This is why we assume that trusting God means the same thing as doing nothing. Pharaoh's voice distorts God's words in our hearts. Instead of doing nothing, however, God's invitation to be still means

---

[53] Ex 5:17.

to rest in the contemplative awareness of God's Presence. It means to prioritize the relationship with Him over everything else, including the effects of that relationship. We live for Him, and from that "living for" comes communion, joy, and wonder. The temptation is to prioritize the effects of relationship with God over the relationship itself. God, it seems, does not work fast enough. So we set aside the simple living-in-relationship for the fruits that should come from it.

Is this not exactly what we hope to achieve from our devices? Do we not look to them to remove from our lives the effects of sin (awareness of death, separation from others, toil and sadness)? We abandon resting in God so that we can have the fruits of that rest at our disposal, without needing to rely on the relationship for them. And yet all we have done instead is strengthen the chains of our imprisonment to sin.

This is why St. Thomas Aquinas says that *acedia* is opposed to the third commandment, by which we are enjoined to rest in God. According to him, the opposite of laziness is not hard work but the joyful offering of self to God in love; and this self-offering itself flows out of the encounter with God in contemplation. On the Lord's Day, the faithful turn their eyes towards the salvation won by Jesus Christ and unite themselves to His own self-offering to the Father. This is not laziness, but is rather the fullness of life.

St. Ignatius of Antioch, a first-century bishop and martyr, describes Christians as those who are "living in accordance with the Lord's Day." Pope Benedict XVI explains that this "means living in the awareness of the liberation brought by Jesus Christ and making our lives a constant self-offering to God, so that his victory may be fully revealed to all humanity through a profoundly renewed existence."[54] The more we turn our eyes to the Lord, the more his own loving sacrifice comes to life within our hearts. "I have been crucified with Christ," says St. Paul, "and the life I now live is not my own; Christ is living in me. The life I live now in the flesh I live by faith in the Son of God who loved me and gave Himself for me."[55]

---

[54] Pope Benedict XVI, *Sacramentum Caritatis* (Vatican City: Libreria Editrice Vaticana, 2007), no. 72.

[55] Gal 2:20.

Christ lives in the hearts of those who live by faith. All we have to do is get out of the way. "With what procrastinations do you wait," St. John of the Cross asks himself, "since from this very moment you can love God in your heart?"[56]

Conclusion

Our screens have turned our eyes towards ourselves, imprisoning us in a sad and dreary world where nothing much amazes us. We have numbed ourselves to reality and become boring and lifeless people. Jesus, however, by his Passion, Death, and Resurrection, has so united Himself to us that He can be found even in our state of imprisonment. The opposite of the person imprisoned by *acedia*, then, is not merely a hard worker. Nor is it someone whose own self-discipline has kept him in control of his life. It is, instead, the person who has *seen something*. And this vision has given him life. It is the one who has turned his eyes towards Jesus and has let the Lord live

---

[56] St. John of the Cross, "Sayings of Light and Love" in *The Collected Works of St. John of the Cross*, 87.

His Life within him. Pope Benedict XVI wrote that "[b]eing a Christian is not the result of an ethical choice or a lofty idea, but the encounter with an event, a person, which gives life a new horizon and a decisive direction."[57] The Christian is the one who has seen the Lord come to him in his own poverty. And the person who lives from that encounter, that is, the person who lives in accordance with the Lord's Day, is the one who has been set free from *acedia*'s kingdom.

---

[57] Pope Benedict XVI, *Deus Caritas Est* (Washington, D.C.: United States Conference of Catholic Bishops, 2005) 1.

Conclusion

Towards the end of *The Two Towers*, the main characters, Frodo and Sam, find themselves on the border of the Enemy's Kingdom. There they are, two halflings of the Shire, two simple hobbits of the quiet countryside, "expected to find a way where the great ones could not go, or dared not go."[58] It seems absurd, these two little people confronting the vast empire of the seemingly all-powerful Enemy. Reflecting on this turn of fate that came into their lives, Sam remarks:

> We shouldn't be here at all, if we'd known more about it before we started. But I suppose it's often that way. The brave things in the old tales and songs, Mr. Frodo: adventures, as I used to call them. I used to think that they were things the wonderful folk of the stories went out and looked for, because they wanted

---

[58] J.R.R. Tolkien, *The Lord of the Rings: The Two Towers* (New York: Ballantine Books, 1982), 297.

> them, because they were exciting and life was a bit dull, a kind of sport, as you might say. But that's not the way of it with the tales that really mattered, or the ones that stay in the mind. Folk seem to have been just landed in them, usually - their paths were laid that way, as you put it. But I suppose they had lots of chances, like us, of turning back, only they didn't. And if they had, we shouldn't know because they'd have been forgotten. We hear about those as just went on...[59]

Sam's words penetrate the mystery of what makes up an adventurous life. A life that we consider exciting does not originate from one's own will. We do not "plan" an exciting life. It originates from another. We *find* ourselves in an adventure; we "land" in one. All that matters on our end is our response.

I began this book with Screwtape's complaint about how bland Hell's fare is these days as they consume the souls of the damned. The noonday devil has successfully neutered modern man's spirit, locking

---

[59] Ibid., 378.

him safely within the confines of his own neatly-ordered world. We may complain that this world is boring, but as long as we have our screens to distract us (or to conjure up manufactured sources of excitement), what matter? The Enemy seems to have imprisoned us impenetrably within his Kingdom.

What the Enemy fails to see is that by imprisoning us here, he has accidentally provided God with a new theme for our Lord to weave into the love song He is continually singing. Jesus, perpetually joining Himself to the history of man, transforms our lives into an adventure by incorporating us into His life. Through the Incarnation, we have "landed in" the story of God's love for man. Our apathy and sadness are part of the divine love song whose discordant notes of the Passion are resolved in the Resurrection's triumphal chorus of eternal happiness and praise. Through Christ, and with Him, and in Him, our lives become far from boring; they become sources of wonder for all with the eyes to see God at work. What matters for us is our response to God's activity: do we persevere in faith? Do we let God act in us? Or are we too concerned with getting ourselves out of Hell that we fail to let Him save us?

The invitation of this book has been to let Christ's own Life, Death, and Resurrection be manifest in our imprisonment, in our own personal Hell. In Matthew's Gospel, we hear of Jesus' rejection by the wise and the learned. Matthew recounts that after this rejection, Jesus "responded" in praise to His Father for having revealed the divine wisdom not to these, but rather to the child-like. Matthew's phrase that Jesus "responded" seems intentional. Leiva-Merikakis comments that it is a curious term, since Jesus had not been replying to any previous comment. According to this commentator, this term reveals the interior life of Christ. His insights are worth quoting at length:

> If Jesus is said to *respond*, it is because, with this passage, we become the privileged witnesses of the divine dialogue of love that is continually developing between Father and Son and that constitutes the very substance of the interior life of God....
>
> For Jesus *to be Son means, essentially, to be response*, and his prayer reveals the tremendously creative power of being depen-

dent on another and responsible to another out of love, as Jesus is with regard to his Father....

We can hardly exaggerate the importance of realizing that this passage not only portrays one episode in the Gospel narrative but reveals Jesus' *ordinary consciousness* of himself as exclusive Son of the eternal God by nature. This prayer, which opens itself up to us *in medias res*, as an interior activity perpetually ongoing in the soul of Jesus, imposes itself as constitutive of the very substance of his being. As such, it provides the essential basis on which to understand *all* of Jesus' deeds and words in the Gospel. This intimate dialogue of love and thanksgiving between Jesus and his Father is the indelible watermark underlying every page of the Gospel, the *basso continuo* supporting every line of the melody that the Savior sings in order to enchant the heart of man.[60]

---

[60] Erasmo Leiva-Merikakis, *Fire of Mercy, Heart of the Word: Meditations on the Gospel According to Saint*

This life of perpetual interior dialogue between Father and Son is, in fact, the very life that Jesus offers us. Jesus sets us free from the isolation of our digital imprisonment by turning that imprisonment into a dialogue between us and the Father. The "intimate dialogue of love" which is the indelible watermark of Christ's life is also the watermark of our lives. It strengthens us to remain attuned to the Father's voice rather than to the cacophonous voices of the world, screaming at us from our devices. It allows us to live in wonder; to live with the perpetual foretaste of Heaven even while on our way to Heaven.

Matthew, Volume One (San Francisco: Ignatius Press, 1996), 685-686.

Made in the USA
Middletown, DE
09 December 2022